Human/
Animal

Life Writing Series

WILFRID LAURIER UNIVERSITY PRESS'S LIFE WRITING series celebrates life writing as both genre and critical practice. As a home for innovative scholarship in theory and critical practice, the series embraces a range of theoretical and methodological approaches, from literary criticism and theory to autoethnography and beyond, and encourages intersectional approaches attentive to the complex interrelationships between gender, class, race, ethnicity, sexuality, ability, and more. In its commitment to life writing as genre, the series incorporates a range of life writing practices and welcomes creative scholarship and hybrid forms. The Life Writing series recognizes the diversity of languages, and the effects of such languages on life writing practices within the Canadian context, including the languages of migration and translation. As such, the series invites contributions from voices and communities who have been under- or misrepresented in scholarly work.

Series editors:
Marlene Kadar, York University
Sonja Boon, Memorial University

Human/ Animal

a bestiary in essays

Amie Souza Reilly

WITH ILLUSTRATIONS BY THE AUTHOR

WILFRID LAURIER
UNIVERSITY PRESS

Wilfrid Laurier University Press acknowledges the support of the Canada Council for the Arts for our publishing program. We acknowledge the financial support of the Government of Canada through the Canada Book Fund for our publishing activities. Funding provided by the Government of Ontario and the Ontario Arts Council. This work was supported by the Research Support Fund.

Library and Archives Canada Cataloguing in Publication

Title: Human/animal : a bestiary in essays / Amie Souza Reilly.
Names: Reilly, Amie Souza, author.
Series: Life writing series.
Description: Series statement: Life writing series | Includes bibliographical references.
Identifiers: Canadiana (print) 20240494350 | Canadiana (ebook) 2024049279X | ISBN 9781771126809 (softcover) | ISBN 9781771126816 (EPUB) | ISBN 9781771126823 (PDF)
Subjects: LCSH: Reilly, Amie Souza. | LCSH: Interpersonal conflict. | LCSH: Human-animal relationships. | LCSH: Violence. | LCSH: Neighbors. | LCSH: Instinct. | LCSH: Regret. | LCGFT: Essays.
Classification: LCC HM1116 .R45 2025 | DDC 303.6—dc23

Cover and interior design by Michel Vrana. Front cover image iStock.

© 2025 Wilfrid Laurier University Press
Waterloo, Ontario, Canada
www.wlupress.wlu.ca

This book is printed on FSC® certified paper. It contains recycled materials and other controlled sources, is processed chlorine-free, and is manufactured using biogas energy. Printed in Canada

Wilfrid Laurier University Press is located on the Haldimand Tract, part of the traditional territories of the Haudenosaunee, Anishnaabe, and Neutral Peoples. This land is part of the Dish with One Spoon Treaty between the Haudenosaunee and Anishnaabe Peoples and symbolizes the agreement to share, to protect our resources, and not to engage in conflict. We are grateful to the Indigenous Peoples who continue to care for and remain interconnected with this land. Through the work we publish in partnership with our authors, we seek to honour our local and larger community relationships, and to engage with the diversity of collective knowledge integral to responsible scholarly and cultural exchange.

To my husband, always.

To my son, best most forever.

*And to the memory of Kiwi Noodle,
the most perfect nonhuman animal
we have ever known.*

People speak sometimes about the "bestial"
cruelty of man, but that is terribly unjust and
offensive to beasts, no animal could ever be so cruel
as a man, so artfully, so artistically cruel.
—FYODOR DOSTOYEVSKY,
translated by Constance Garnett

People are trapped in history, and
history is trapped in them.
—JAMES BALDWIN

In a house besieged lived a man and a woman.
From where they cowered in the kitchen the man
and woman heard small explosions. "The wind,"
said the woman. "Hunters," said the man.
"The rain," said the woman. "The army," said
the man. The woman wanted to go home, but
she was already home, there in the middle
of the country in a house besieged.
—LYDIA DAVIS, "In a House Besieged"

Table of Contents

Author's note

AMONG OTHER THINGS, THIS IS A BOOK ABOUT NAMES and naming—the etymology of certain animal names, Linnaeus's classifications, the erasure of names belonging to the enslaved, the harm of name-calling.

The people in this story are real, though most of their names have been changed or omitted. Because this both is and isn't his story, my son is only referred to as "my child" or "my son." I have used my husband's real name. Because they are innocent and this is my version of events, the names of our neighbors—the ones who are not the sole focus of this book—have been changed. The names of the brothers who lived next door have been changed as well, not because they are innocent, but to protect all parties and their families from harmful exposure.

Preface

The first book I ever wrote was about dinosaurs. I began by drawing them, and then, beneath each drawing, I listed facts I'd copied from flashcards. I was no more than six. When I finished, I stapled the pages together—a bestiary of the prehistoric.

During an early draft of what eventually became this book, two friends gifted me a copy of T. J. Elliott's translation of the thirteenth century's *A Medieval Bestiary*. There are no dinosaurs inside, but rather animals and birds, both real and imagined. Gillian Tyler illustrated it with wood engravings, rendering each animal in lines so wild they almost appear woven from grass.

In the introduction, Elliott defines the *Medieval Bestiary* as a book that "really tells us more about human beings and the history of ideas than about natural history."

He says this because each entry begins with a poetic description of the animal's nature, descriptions rooted in author perception rather than reality. Beneath these descriptions, allegories align human behaviors with the animals just explained. The resulting pattern of "facts" supported by stories makes accessible animals most readers would never otherwise see, either because of the impossibility of traveling to their habitats, as in the case of the elephant, or, as in the case of the mermaid, the impossibility of their existence.

This medieval bestiary's human-centered Christian moralizing feels familiar. In America, moralizing politicians sometimes warp and weaponize doctrine, discounting the people living outside their belief system. They twist the language and ignore it, plowing through the boundary between church and state, hurling insults like baseballs. As an American, I am as fluent in this behavior as I am in American English.

My fluency in these aspects of our culture and language is likely how I arrived at the idea for the bestiary entries that appear in the chapters you are about to read.

The animal entries in these pages, like those in Elliott's book, are also more about understanding the human condition than the animals themselves, though many include biological facts and historical anecdotes. However, even those are meant to relate the animal to the human reading about them. Taken collectively, there's a larger point to be made.

What I mean is, in the English language, dozens of animal names are also used as verbs. And very often, almost always, these words refer to acts of violence, labor, or motherhood. *To badger, to hawk, to bear.* Within the story I am about to tell, you'll find my own sketches of these animals alongside etymological summaries of the verb usages of that animal's name, which I've sourced from the *Oxford English Dictionary.* Etymologies are histories, and, as James Geary notes in *I Is an Other,* full of metaphor.

The English language, like the English colonialism that spread to America, is full of brutality. So then, using animal names to mean verbs of harm, labor, and mothering becomes a metaphor and an analogy for the power baked into our white patriarchal imperialist society, with its violence, destructive capitalist practices, and its laws and medical policies that do very little to support mothers.

These bestiary entries appear within a story about my neighbors. For the first few years we lived here, the two brothers living next door threatened my family in a variety of ways, trying to get us to move out of our house so they could buy it instead. I see them, too, as symbolic of an American culture built on harm. In their desire for control and conquest are the roots of American history, its patriarchal white settler colonizer violence.

A bestiary catalogs mystery, organizes the unknown, puzzles out wonder. I've written a catalog, too—of animals and insects, but also wrongdoings, books I've read, movies I've seen, childhood memories, and history. A bestiary of possible reasons for my neighbors' actions and my reactions.

When I was six and making books about dinosaurs, I wrote and drew at my parents' dining room table. Now, when I can, I write outside in our backyard, and I text my husband whenever I see animal activity. *A chipmunk ran across the top of the fence! A hummingbird is hovering over the zinnias!* Today I heard a quick rustle in the overgrown holly bush and looked up just in time to see a hawk swoop out with a small brown bird in their beak.

Animals do not interrupt my story; they are the story.

The bestiary entries inside this book pause the narrative, but do not disrupt it. Instead, they supplement, support, and expand this story into one of past and present, language and image. There are so many ways to write about violence.

But in the violence is also a search for gentleness. In the opening pages of his bestiary, Elliott dedicates his translation to the memory of his mother. He writes, "One of the earliest of many tender recollections which I cherish is of her reading stories of animals to me."

Come with me, and let me tell you an animal story.

I. What happened

to badger/to ape

IN LATE AUGUST 2014, WE MOVED INTO AN OLD WHITE house with green shutters. It was within walking distance to the station where I and my husband would catch our daily trains. The middle school my six-year-old would someday attend was also down the street, a selling point that back then seemed like a far-off future, but now that he is older seems like an impossible past. This house has hardwood floors and leaded glass windows. The ropes inside the windows snapped ages ago, so we hold them open with thick sticks. You can feel the horsehair in the plaster walls if you run your hand over certain spots. There is a bedroom at either end of the hallway upstairs, and a tiny office with a pull-string light. Outside, a patio laid from old bricks and two walnut trees held up a hammock. The beach is nearby, only a very long walk or a moderate bike ride away. In *The Sea Around Us*, Rachel Carson writes, "Beginnings are apt to be shadowy." I had just gotten remarried and was about to start graduate school.

For the first three years we lived here, we were stalked.

The men following us were brothers. They had grown up in and still owned, though no longer lived in, the little yellow house with which we shared a driveway. Jim spoke slowly and deliberately and wore gray-tinted glasses. Wes had a ponytail curling out from beneath a dark blue baseball hat. He spoke in chaos—repetitive, jumpy, and self-congratulatory. Both were White, tall, and in their sixties. They drove a silver Buick Century.

We were returning from a walk the first time we caught them in our driveway, standing close to our house, arms crossed and waiting for us as if we'd broken curfew. Days before, in a lawyer's office, after we'd signed the papers and held the keys to our new house, our real estate agent told us these neighbors were *nosy, but mostly harmless*. Did she emphasize *mostly*? In our driveway, they introduced themselves with their hands out, walking closer and closer to us. Wes pointed at their yellow house and said, *This is the house that was built for us*, then Jim followed with, *We know all the families who've ever lived in your house*, and then one of them said, *We gave Jerry that statue in your backyard*. I didn't realize we'd been walking backward. By the time they stopped talking, they had backed us up against our door.

I am a woman who often feels afraid around men. My fear is gut-deep, learned through culture and history and also from my mother. I anticipate feeling afraid, or at least wary, in meeting rooms and in bars and on elevators and in parking garages because these are places where I have been shouted at, leered at, groped, and followed. But I did not expect to feel this kind of fear in my new house with my new husband. This house is on a street I had driven down countless times before, in a town I had already lived in for fifteen years. My husband had been my boyfriend for several years before we'd married. The familiarity of city, street, and partner were a comfort. The familiarity of fear, though familiar, was unexpected. "Fluency in fear—and making us police ourselves—is how women are kept in check," writes Pumla Dineo Gqola.[1] Even with my back against our house, as Matt opened the door and hurriedly let us in, I smiled at the brothers, nodded, and said, *It is so nice to meet you.*

⊙ ⊙ ⊙

Our house is nearly 150 years old. This means it wasn't possible for Wes and Jim to have known all the families who'd lived here before us. As they backed us into our door, Wes told us they also knew where we had lived before. *The way you decorated*, he said, *we can tell you are good people.* (I would have thought, *There is too much subjectivity to correlate a person's "goodness" with their art*, but they were standing so close to me.) We realized, after we told them we had to go, after we opened the door enough to get inside, after we closed and locked ourselves in, that this was another impossible claim. We had not lived together before. Whose house had they seen? Whether it was Matt's house or mine, in order for the brothers to have seen the rooms we'd lived in, they could have come to an open house. Or worse, they peered in the windows. Imagine two faces pressed against locked glass. The boldness of daytime voyeurism.

Badger: v. To haggle, drive a bargain. Also, to pester, to bother, to ply with repeated and irritating requests to do something. Probably an allusion to the baiting of badgers by humans. (See also *fish*, also *clam*.) Uses of *badger* in the seventeenth century allude to the supposed tenacity of the animal's bite, gripping so hard its teeth meet.

I am not guiltless in the act of snooping. I have scrolled strangers' social media accounts, have googled the names of people I am about to meet, or have recently met, or would like to someday meet. I've peeked through cracks in doors, pressed my ear against a wall to hear private conversations. The difference between their voyeurism and mine is I never told those I spied on what I had done. I knew to keep my acts a secret. *Nosy, but mostly harmless.* But Wes and Jim told us they had seen inside one of our houses, had copped to their nosiness. That could only mean they wanted us to know they had been looking.

In her book *Staring: How We Look*, Rosemarie Garland-Thomson writes "...staring at once provokes and paralyzes its object, eliciting both anger and anxiety."[2] Once inside our house, my fists clenched and ready, I wanted to hit them. For the rest of the evening, I worried over curtains—we hadn't bought any yet. We rifled through unpacked boxes, found towels, a few blankets, some nails, and a hammer and covered up all the windows.

Garland-Thomson goes on to write about staring as an act of dominance, enforcing social hierarchies and regulating access to resources. Here is a conversation I dismissed when it first happened: Just after we put in the offer to buy this house, before we received word the sellers accepted, our real estate agent called. She said another bid had come in, higher, and in cash. We could not offer more money and did not have that kind of cash. We were nervous. We did not have a backup plan. And then, overnight, we got the all clear. *The current homeowners are not interested in selling to anyone else.* We mistook this as a sign of good luck. In our gratitude, we did not ask questions.

The day after our neighbors' forceful introduction, they came back. I saw them in the yard when I left to catch my train. It was shortly after lunch. My classes all happened in the evenings, in the Bronx, a two-hour train ride away. I waved to them but quickened my steps. Wes shouted at my back as I walked away. *We offered*

Jerry more money for that house, you know. And we offered him cash.
He paused, waited for me to react, but I did not turn around. For
a moment, I did not move at all; no fight or flight, only freeze. *But
they didn't like us. They said they like you better.* The brothers' first
attempt to own this house was to buy us out, and though it failed,
it was quickly clear they were not ready to give up. I didn't know
how to respond to Wes, so I left. I got on my train and went to
class. When I returned home, I found a note from them in our
mailbox taped to a small gift bag. Inside the bag, a candleholder
from IKEA. Inside the card, they had written: *Congratulations
Reilly family! May God bless your home.* I threw it all away.

We didn't see them every day. Mostly they lived in another town.
In a house like yours. But bigger. Much bigger, they told us. Another
flex of strength. (Did I look it up? Of course. I saw on Google Street
View that it was a very large colonial, new construction. White like
ours, but without shutters. Dozens of small American flags lined
the garden and the walkway.) But at least once a week, they arrived
next door. Several times, we caught them walking the perimeter of
our backyard. Once, they lifted the lid and poked through our compost bin. During every visit, I watched them pluck at invisible tufts
of grass in their front lawn until their plastic solar lights flicked on.
After the grass, they picked up sticks, from their yard and ours, and
then dumped the small twig-piles across the street, beneath a tree at
the end of another neighbor's driveway.

They learned our schedules quickly and pulled into their driveway twice a week at the same time I left to walk to the bus stop at
the end of my son's school day. When I started picking him up at
school instead, I saw their silver Buick drive past us as we pulled
into the doughnut shop. At home in our living room, whenever
something cut across the outside light and cast a shadow on the
porch, we froze, hair on end, eyes widened, and listened.

Their car's loose muffler rumbled. I could hear when it crested
the hill—a warning, and so my ears stayed tuned. Here's Gqola

again, on female fear: "This heightened vigilance requires that women consider how they will fight back, or modify their behaviour, to try and remain safe." Running up to our attic, where the air was hot and dusty with exposed insulation, I watched them, unseen, from a small window. As I looked down, I questioned what they were capable of, worried whether we were safe. *Mostly harmless*, the real estate agent had said. *They are a little odd*, the previous owners told us. But if that's all they were, then why did my skin go slick whenever I heard them pull up?

For the nine hundred forty-three days we lived next to them, I was always waiting for them to arrive. As I waited, I imagined what it would feel like to close Wes's hands in my car door or hit him with sacks of oranges. I thought about running them over, or spraying their driveway with water and letting it freeze so Jim would slip and fall. Even though I have always hated guns, one night, I sat on our couch and started a whisper-debate with my husband about getting one, just in case.

I felt afraid, though for the first few months we lived here the reason for my fear was hard to pinpoint. In the beginning, there were no overt threats, but they stood too close, said peculiar things, stood in our yard uninvited and stared. Back then, I felt I should be able to dismiss these behaviors, that though I felt something off, I could have been overreacting. But the language in those warnings from the agent and Jerry felt coded, couched; *mostly harmless, a little strange.*

Even if I wasn't immediately certain why I was afraid of them, I recognized my physical reactions to them. I hesitated to say hello, felt a yawning pit in my gut when I saw them. I always wanted to know when they were outside and then, when they did arrive, I'd shut all the windows. These were feelings I'd had before, moves I'd made in other situations in order to avoid men I'd perceived to be threatening. From Gqola: "Patriarchy runs on fear, fear of being an outsider, fear of being brutalized, fear of being too much, too inadequate, too vocal, or too different."[3]

The hold they had over me was recognizable because it was familiar. And the more I watched them, it became clear that they saw themselves as a team—the two of them against the neighborhood, perhaps even me, specifically. The smirks, the repetitive door slamming, the dumped yard waste, the positions of their bodies as they stood in our yard and stared appeared to be strategic moves, as if they came here to play a game where only they knew the rules. French writer and filmmaker Virginie Despentes wrote that the exclusion of women's bodies is the foundation masculinity is built upon, because it is in such moments "that their famous male bonding takes place."[4] Men together hold more potential for violence than a man alone.

When bell hooks wrote about a group of White men she observed walking in front of her in New Haven, she noticed how they become louder and stronger in a group. As she listened to them talk and categorize the women they had sex with, she also noticed how they "claim the body of the colored Other instrumentally, as unexplored terrain, a symbolic frontier that will be fertile ground for their reconstruction of the masculine norm."[5] Not only a game of exclusion, but conquest. hooks' language evokes images of westward-driving settler colonizers. The women those young men were talking about rendered not as human beings, but as property, like land to be stood upon, claimed, owned. They hadn't even noticed bell hooks walking behind them.

Racism and sexism, as well as classism and ableism, intersect to perpetuate the power dynamics implicit in the brotherhood Despentes and hooks describe. Anyone outside of that brotherhood of straight, White, able-bodied men of some financial comfort becomes feminized, mocked, dominated, dubbed as Other. Before seeing us, Jim and Wes assumed economic superiority, tried to outbid us on our house. A year later, Wes tried to embarrass my husband with homophobic taunts. When they learned of my previous divorce, they repeatedly mentioned it as a failure of my character. In 2019, in a tweet echoing the ways men have been calling women hysterical, Donald Trump told teen climate activist Greta Thunberg to "work on her anger management problem" after she won *Time* Magazine's Person of the Year award.[6] In 2022, Kentucky senator Mitch McConnell voted against legislation that would protect interracial marriage.[7] In August 2023, Texas governor Greg Abbott placed a row of buoys affixed with sawblades into the Rio Grande to maim anyone attempting to climb over the border.[8] There is a comradery in cruelty.

◎ ◎ ◎

Whenever the brothers arrived, they brought stuff—boxes of Entenmann's baked goods, stacks of newspapers and magazines. Once, I came home from the post office and there was a three-foot-tall stuffed banana propped against their garage. Each holiday, they put a new wreath on the door and a new garland on the railing. Nothing ever came back out of their house. I am reminded of the Great Pacific Garbage Patch off the coast of California, that floating tangle of plastic that will never go away, large enough to be seen from space. They never rolled out the bins on trash night, never moved the filthy car parked in their garage out into the light.

Even though I watched them carry brown paper bags and canvas totes up their three front steps and inside their front door while thinking of and planning their deaths, (if not oranges, then perhaps a sock filled with loose change) I had also tried, *we* had also tried, to show them kindness. As if good deeds might work as a shield. The first winter we lived here, we cleared the snow from their driveway. I waved when I saw them outside, though averted my eyes from theirs. We said hellohowareyou quickly when they walked past us with fists full of sticks. All acts of self-preservation, kindnesses like stiffened elbows to keep them at arm's length. But if we were only pretending to be nice to avoid getting yelled at, does that diminish our acts?

Ape: v. To imitate, to mimic (pretentiously, irrationally, or absurdly). To mimic the reality. (See also *parrot*.)

It is strange to write about feeling trapped in my house, afraid of our neighbors, given that we are living with a virus that had, when it began, kept us sequestered inside for so long, afraid of everyone. In the early days of the COVID-19 pandemic, as my family tried to adjust to endless time indoors, I grew feral with worry. When we could, we bought groceries in bulk, wiped them down with hand sanitizer and put them in empty coolers in the basement. We were squirreling away food. Upstairs, in an attempt to make us feel safe even if we weren't, I piled the living room couch with blankets and pillows. Like a nest. It was during those first bleak days when I began making a list of all the animal names we use as verbs.[9] The list became our family game. In the middle of eating dinner, or watching television, or taking a masked walk around the block, someone would shout out *Peacock! Ferret!* Upstairs, in our shared office, I looked up each animal in my *OED*, taking notes in the order we thought of them. And then I noticed something. Almost every animal, when reconsidered into its verb form, defines an act of violence, labor, or motherhood.

The violence of these verbs is, at times, overt. *To bat, to ram, and to slug* are all verbs connected to hitting. There is also *to goose,* which means to grab someone, likely in the rear, likely without consent. These are verbs of attack.

Then there are verbs like *to fish* and *to hawk,* which are verbs tied to labor. These are words of work. Additionally, the verb forms of these animal names often mean the hunting of themselves. We can see this not only in *to fish,* but also *to clam* and *to louse.* How often, especially under our American capitalism, is labor an act of violence? *To hawk* used to mean to hunt with falcons, but more commonly we use it to mean *to sell.* We also use *to squirrel* with *away* as a way of saying *to store.* Other verbs, like *to hog, to wolf,* and *to swallow* are connected to the act of eating, and therefore consumption, which brings us right back to labor and violence.

Labor is also connected to motherhood, both in the birth processes we call labor, and in the invisible work of mothering. The word *labor* itself means *to work* and *to endure pain or suffer.* Verbs like *to bear* are often used to describe childbirth, as in *to bear a child,* but we also use *to bear* in relation to guns, as in *to bear arms.* Nowadays*, to pig* is mostly used with *out,* as in *to pig out,* which we use to mean *to gorge oneself,* but *to pig* once also meant to give birth, though it was used derogatorily. There is violence in these mother-verbs, too, not just because of the inherent blood and pain of birth, but also in the statistics. According to a 2023 *PBS News Hour* podcast, the maternal mortality rate among Black women in America in the same year was nearly 70 deaths for every 100,000 live births, which is 2.6 times the rate for White women, regardless of income or education.[10] America is a country without maternal leave or universal health care, but with endlessly increasing costs for childcare. More recently and with growing frequency, motherhood is a value signifier; politicians argue that a woman's purpose is tied to motherhood and stay-at-home moms with seemingly endless wealth become social media influencers, while the right to abortion in many states has been restricted or banned.[11]

Taken collectively, these verbs become metaphors. Although the use of animals in language—as metaphors, dual noun/verbs, and idioms—isn't unique to English, as I look up each of these words in the *OED*, I can't help but think about how the British came here and spread their white violence everywhere. The language I speak is the language of violent power. These animal verbs seem to be a perfect representation of that power.

This is also how I see my neighbors.

Though at first I wasn't sure why I was afraid, their behavior escalated to more overt acts of violence, of invasion and boundary crossing. My fear was validated, even when I called it into question. And as they threatened, stalked, and shouted at us, something else became clear—their behavior, though troubling, scary even, was not unique. They are just like many other neighbors throughout history and in other American suburbs.

In the introduction to *Animalia: An Anti-Imperial Bestiary for Our Times*, Antoinette Burton and Renisa Mawani write of rhinos goring men along the new railway lines the British cut through Uganda in the nineteenth century. A rhino's double horns and thick skin look like armor, their small eyes surrounded by wrinkles, like a grandmother's. Up until the arrival of the British, they had been grazing their land in large numbers. What some call progress, others know as harm. Burton and Mawani explain the rhinoceroses' behavior as protest: "Animals regularly disrupted imperial agendas by defying taxonomies and categories imposed by the British on the natural world."[12] Perhaps a vestigial belief from the divine right of kings, the British imperialists may have been intent on their believed superiority, but the rhinos reacted with defiance, protective of their home.

◉ ◉ ◉

I tried to write about Jim and Wes before, once in a novel that went nowhere, and then in several essays, each one worse than the last. *Mom, why are you always looking out the window?* my son would ask when I peered through the curtains for the millionth time. Whenever they mowed into our yard, went through our compost bin, stood in our driveway, or followed us through town, I felt an urge to scream, to run outside and confront them, push them back onto their own lawn. I felt I needed to somehow protect my family, though I knew I couldn't leave my six-year-old inside while I went chasing after them. That would be at best frivolous, at worst dangerous. I did not know yet what they were capable of. *Just checking to see*, I'd answer, letting the sentence trail off.

Each time I wrote about them before was an attempt to think through what had happened. But I couldn't get the words right. How does anyone write about fear, or powerlessness, or motherhood? How can I write about all three?

I sat on my office couch upstairs to write down each animal definition, then on the living room couch downstairs to draw them. Perhaps the bestiary came from a vestigial impulse, somewhat scrambled, from the British imperialist lineage I inherited from my mother's side. In a box in the attic where I went to watch my neighbors, there is a thick stack of paper held together with a binder clip inside a worn-out yellow envelope.[13] On those pages, my mother's history is outlined, the long list of names and dates typed beneath a poorly drawn attempt at a family crest. That trail stretches back to a famous ship that landed in Massachusetts centuries ago. Though I understand Wes and Jim as embodiments and products of white patriarchal structures, I must not forget that it is in me, too. But maybe I am moved to create a bestiary because it is a hybrid text, an "aesthetic object with a pedagogical purpose,"[14] which is a way to learn through art. In order to comprehend the brothers' actions and also understand my reactions, I needed more than a retelling of events, more than a story. I can think better when I'm writing, see better when I am drawing.

◎ ◎ ◎

One afternoon in those early months of living here, as we got ready to go grocery shopping, my son asked me again why I was looking out the window. The brothers' driveway was empty when we left; however, they were there when we got back. I brought my son into our house without them noticing, but as I started unloading the bags from the trunk they came out of their garage, stared at me as I unpacked our car. Wes rubbed his chin with his thumb until I went inside and closed the curtains. Hours later, I heard them finally leave. When he got home from work, I relayed this story to my husband. I told him, *The way he looked at me, I felt like a piece of meat.*

Carol J. Adams, in *The Sexual Politics of Meat*, argues that meat is a problematic animal metaphor. For women who've been harmed, she says, "...the death experience of animals acts to illustrate the lived experience of women."[15] As in, women who have survived a trauma live with a fear of death that extends beyond themselves, perhaps because they no longer feel like themselves, no longer feel human. And though I think on some level many people, regardless of gender or history of harm, fear death, I am interested in what Adams argues about how the animals in this metaphor become twice erased, first in death and again when their carcasses become stand-ins for the human female body in the aftermath of violence. Why did I say I felt like meat? What is it about meat, specifically, not just the animal, that felt like an apt description? When I used it, it was because I felt like I was about to be eaten.

Paging through the *OED* to look up these animal verbs, I can't help but think about what it means to use colonizer language to represent nonhuman animals. How language can be violent, how mine is a language of exploitation, which means I cannot communicate without harm.

◎ ◎ ◎

The animal entries in this text form a linguistic history within my lived history, not disrupting the text so much as supporting it. There is something I can learn from these animals, how we treat and have treated them, not just corporeally, but in language.

Naming is an act that some claim is specifically human. I might argue, as others have, that we simply do not understand the language of nonhuman animals. Alexis Pauline Gumbs writes of how pregnant dolphins sing to their babies while in utero, and in the weeks after birth, singing becomes a way for the newborns to learn their names. Not only do their mothers sing their names, but "the rest of the pod quiets so that this can happen."[16] But not all acts of naming are gentle. When Swedish botanist, zoologist, taxonomist, and physician Carl Linnaeus dubbed human animals *mammals* in the eighteenth century—despite the fact that only half of us can lactate—he did so in part because he was involved with a campaign to outlaw wet nursing, which, in turn, would keep women in the home.[17] Additionally, his contribution to the categorization of living beings is inextricably tied to Othering. To categorize is to decide who belongs inside and who is left out. Sixty years after Linnaeus, a woman from the British colony on the Cape of Good Hope was taken to London. She was exhibited for audiences in England and Paris, displayed as if in an animal show, studied by zoologists and physiologists looking to compare her, part of "the lowliest race of humans" with "the highest type of ape." Her Dutch name was Saartjie Baartman, her British name was Sarah. Her real name remains unknown.

In racism and in disability, naming is used to brand, erase, make Other, create distance, and make spectacle. When Eli Clare writes of cure and disability, he writes "Defects are disposable and abnormal, body-minds or objects to eradicate."[18] Further down the page, he describes a memory: school bullies calling him names, taunting him by calling him a monkey. "Even as the word *monkey* connected me to the nonhuman natural world, I became supremely unnatural." The distance created here is also linguistic. Name-calling often means using adjectives—someone is weird, or strange, or nerdy, but "monkey," in its noun-ness, replaces Clare's human-ness altogether. Seven weeks after I gave birth, I returned too soon to work.[19] Every two hours, when I left my seat and headed to the closet where I pumped my breast milk into pouches I'd freeze in our communal refrigerator, a male colleague called me *Nature Girl*. Another taped a drawing of a cow to the door.

◎ ◎ ◎

The defiant rhinos of the nineteenth century were no match for British guns. According to the Uganda Wildlife Authority, there are no more rhinos in Uganda. They have been hunted and poached, mostly for their horns. In 2018, east of where the Ugandan rhinos gored those railroad workers centuries ago, the last male white rhinoceros died in Kenya. His name was Sudan. His species has been almost completely wiped out, not just by hunting, but also habitat loss and war. Only Sudan's daughter and granddaughter remain, and although attempts have been made to implant them with fertilized eggs, neither has been able to carry to term. There are three embryos frozen in a lab.[20]

For the first three years we lived in this house—which were also the first three years of my second marriage, the first three years of my child's elementary school education—we were stalked by our neighbors, and we wanted to hurt our neighbors. That first summer and for three summers after, though never on the same date, close to midnight, we'd hear a shout. A man's voice bellowed from a moving car, heading toward the train station. Each one of

his words its own statement: *Fuck. You. Wes.* His shout came as
a shock, followed by dread, and then a heaviness pressed into my
chest. The patriarchy, Gqola tells us, terrorizes women all the time,
but it also brutalizes men.

II. On boundaries

to bear/to pig

YESTERDAY I THOUGHT ABOUT THIS LINE FROM ELI Clare's book *Brilliant Imperfection*: "I feel great turmoil about being human."[1] At the time it crossed my mind, I was reading an article about horseshoe crabs.

Horseshoe crabs have survived the dinosaurs and are native to the shoreline near where I live. Because of the presence of copper, their blood is bright blue. Their blue blood is not only beautiful, but it also clots around bacteria. For over fifty years, scientists have used horseshoe crab blood to test for bacterial endotoxins in drugs, medical devices, and vaccines. Millions of human lives have been saved from contamination by this crab blood toxin-detection system.[2]

One summer, our second or maybe third in this house, we saw a horseshoe crab at the beach, flipped on her back. We stopped to look. We thought she was dead, but then a leg twitched. Gently, carefully, Matt flipped her over. She walked away from where we stood on the exposed sandbar, but turned around before she got too far, scuttled her ragged claws across our feet before finally returning to whatever depths she'd come from. To harvest the blood from these crabs, the companies who bleed them pay fishermen to either trawl the bottom of the sea and drag them up in big nets or grab them from shorelines, sometimes by their tails. Once caught, they are tossed into containers and driven to labs where they are stabbed in the heart, their blue blood drained. In some places, the bled crabs are killed and used as bait. Others are released, though how many survive reentry is impossible to calculate. We know, though, that their population is dwindling. This means that other animals, like a small bird called the red knot, also suffer. Without horseshoe crab eggs, they have nothing to eat. I am thinking about this because I am due soon for another booster of COVID vaccine, and it is likely the safety of that vaccine was tested using horseshoe crab blood. Here is Eli Clare again. "Any reckoning with personhood has to account for this destruction, too."[3]

When I was a child, I believed my blood was blue inside my veins and only became red when it contacted air. The term "blue-blooded" is used to describe someone aristocratic, noble, someone of or from a prominent family. (*We can tell you are good people.*) In the article where I learned about horseshoe crab blood and vaccinations there is a photo: In the background, blurred, are people in lab coats, masks on their faces and paper caps over their hair.[4] In focus, at the foreground is a row of horseshoe crabs on a table, their tails folded beneath them, so they appear halved. Metal tubes poke out from their midpoints, the ends balanced over glass bottles, each one at least half-filled with blue. When trying to ward off harm, we often cause it.

Eula Biss notes in *On Immunity* that the puncture act of an injection can be enough to make some people faint, which means even an act of protection can bring about an unwanted reaction. She also notes that the British call a vaccination a *jab*, but Americans, with our love of guns, call it a *shot*. I am rereading Biss's book at the same time as Clare's, and I imagine using a needle and thread to stitch the two together. "The ableist invention of defectiveness functions as an indisputable justification not only for cure but also for many systems of oppression," Clare writes.[5] *Defective* is an adjective, a name given by able-bodied people to those whose bodies work differently than their own. The able-bodied use this word in the name of "cure," but as Clare argues, "cure" often comes with harm—sometimes that harm manifests in the form of more pain, side effects, or an altered sense of self; other times, this coincides with an Othering, and the able-bodied use the term *defective* to see themselves as superior. Biss wrote her book while thinking about vaccinating her child. Vaccines are a form of protection, a preventive cure for diseases that could cause death or serious illness. But they don't exist without consequences, don't course through our bloodstreams without bringing with them a history of hurt. Cure, I see now, can also be tied to harm.

◎ ◎ ◎

There's a concrete statue of a gargoyle in our backyard that Jim told us they gave to Jerry, the previous owner of this house. Two feet tall with nubbed horns on its head and rounded wings on its back, it crouches with its elbows on its knees. I have seen dozens more just like it in the garden center at the Lowe's Home Improvement store near the mall. A true gargoyle is used as a waterspout, redirecting rainwater off buildings while also warding off evil spirits. The one in our yard does neither. For a long time, we left it right where we'd found it, which was at the end of a mostly overgrown walkway in the backyard that seemed to start from and lead to nowhere. We left it there because we are mildly superstitious and worried that if the brothers had gifted it, then moving it might release something negative. We thought this even though the negative already existed. The path has since completely grown over. Over the last few years, an increase in rainfall has made that part of the yard more susceptible to flooding. Our fear of the gargoyle falling over and breaking into sharp pieces outweighed our previous concerns, so last summer we moved it to a flat spot closer to the house. It peeks out from beneath a hedge that grows behind the couch on the brick patio, where I am writing this right now.

I doubt whether Wes and Jim gave that statue to Jerry. I think he told a lie to trick us into thinking they were good neighbors. They were not good neighbors. They were boundary-breakers. Instigators. Threateners. Stalkers.

◎ ◎ ◎

In Galway Kinnell's poem "The Bear," a hunter baits and follows a bear until he dies. The hunter then cuts into the carcass, eats and drinks from the bear before slicing him open completely and climbing inside him to sleep.[6] I read this poem and think, *Wes and Jim were the hunter and I was their bear.* The years we lived beside Wes and Jim are parasitic inside me, have changed the way I think, the way I move through the world. Each time I hear a voice like Wes's or see a man who stands like Jim, my heart races. I did not go out of my way to avoid confrontation before them, I didn't second-guess the way I act under pressure. I didn't use to lose my breath when a door slams. But now I do.

The poem shifts after the hunter climbs inside the bear's (dead meat) body. In a dream, the hunter then becomes the bear and relives his painful death, "lumbering flatfooted/over the tundra,/ stabbed twice from within." He awakens, he thinks, to witness a different bear, a female bear this time, licking herself clean. If this is an act of remorse, then the similarities between the brothers next door and Kinnell's hunter end here. The final line of "The Bear" leaps to a muddy conclusion about poetry, "what, anyway,/was that sticky infusion, that rank flavor of blood, that poetry, by which I lived?" I cannot tell whether the hunter's killing and then entering is an act of conquest or an attempt to find comfort. At first I thought Wes and Jim wanted to take our house, but what if they were running from their own? And why the gargoyle gift? Why the candle? Bribes for friendship? Gaslighting? Could Kinnell's hunter's post-emergence vision of a female bear be a message about rebirth? What, anyway, is the relationship between language and blood? When the she-bear licks her lumped fur into shapes, is she acting as an artist or a priest?

Bear: v. To carry. From the Gothic *bairam*, in all senses, "to carry, to bring, endure, to give birth."

We bear the weight of; we bear the brunt of. The past tense of *bear* is *bore*, which possibly emerged from the middle English *borne* or *boren*. It is believed by some that *borne* meant carrying weight and *born* meant giving birth. Pregnancy is a weight borne before the baby is born. We bear children. We also bear arms.

When we moved into this house, the part of the yard where ours meets Jim and Wes's was separated only by a cluster of rose of Sharon trees. Every August they bloom lavender, their open pink middles interrupted by fluffy yellow stamens. *Those were my mother's favorite trees*, Jim told me once, and I have disliked them ever since. Although the trees did not stretch the length of our two yards, they made it easy to visualize where our space ended and the brothers' space began. However, a natural margin of trees is not enough, legally speaking, to define the limits of suburban spaces, so there was also a survey stick—a metal rod, spray-painted orange at the tip, jutting straight out of the ground behind a small hill where a crabapple tree had been hollowed by termites. On their lawn-cutting days, Jim pushed his mower through the tree border and into our yard, further and further, closer and closer to the dead crabapple tree and then beyond it. Wes followed behind him with a rake. They left the mower running as they looked up and into our windows. They moved my son's toys, kicked the dog's tennis balls from one end of the yard to the other. The day they pulled the survey stick from the ground, they leaned it against the backside of the dead tree.

We found it on a Saturday. Our six-year-old was using the hill to learn to ride his bike without training wheels. We called the police because we weren't sure who else to call and felt that something illegal had happened. An officer came to our house, wrote down what we said. He filed a report, very official, and we received a copy. I put it in an envelope and stuffed it in a drawer in the sideboard.

The survey stick was just a piece of rebar, brownish, about the same diameter as a nickel. But pulled from where it had once jutted out from an overgrown shrub and propped instead against that tree trunk, it became at once ineffective and menacing. Because we had not seen them do it, the police officer said there was no way to prove Wes and Jim had been the ones who removed it. Though they did make a phone call to Wes, a follow up to our complaint. Wes told them that we were the ones who pulled it. That we were trying to frame him. For what, I am uncertain.

When Hannah Arendt wrote about the distinction between the morality of men and the immortality of nature, she also talked about the writing of history. "All things that owe their existence to men, such as works, deeds, and words, are perishable, infected, as it were, by the mortality of their authors."[7] Here is a list of boundaries: a piece of metal in the ground, a cluster of trees, a paper blueprint drawn up years ago. The property marker and paper plan this plot of land is drawn on are temporary, their meaning rotting as I sit on the couch in front of the gargoyle, facing the line of rose of Sharon trees. I watch a brown cardinal lift from a branch that has not yet bloomed. She flies straight up, and I lose sight of her in the glare of the sun.

◎ ◎ ◎

The original police report from that day was likely filed in a cabinet at the police station, and the deed outlining the divide between our yard and Jim and Wes's is likely kept in a drawer inside a building in the center of town. The putting away of seemingly important things inside drawers reminds me of my favorite fragment in *Roland Barthes on Roland Barthes*. After a piece of his rib is removed, the surgeon gives Barthes the bone, wrapped in gauze like a gift. Even though it is his—"my body belongs to me" he writes—Barthes, unsure what to do with it, tosses the bone into a drawer, where it rattles around with old keys and a report card. It stays there until the day he throws it out a window. Kinnell's hunter in "The Bear" wraps a rib, too. In order to kill the bear, he wraps a wolf's rib in blubber (the wolf's rib does not belong to him) and leaves it for the bear, who eats it not knowing that once the blubber is digested, the sharp point of the bone will slowly kill him from the inside. Like "The Bear," Barthes's narrative also ends in a vision. Where Kinnell's hunter imagines he sees a bear licking herself, Barthes imagines he tosses his rib out a window as if "scattering his own ashes." I believed I knew this Barthes segment by heart, but it turns out I misremembered. I thought Barthes imagined a dog coming along to *eat* his rib, and I wanted to write about feeling like meat, about death and weapons and boundaries, but the imaginary dog does not eat Barthes's rib, he only sniffs it. There is no consumption, only rejection.

◎ ◎ ◎

The boundary that Jim and Wes crossed, the boundary of back-yards, made me feel powerless while it rendered them powerful. When they pulled the survey stick, it became weapon-like in that it removed the symbol that should have been understood as a bound-ary—a line not to be crossed. The reason these sticks exist at all is to determine the size of a yard, the monetary value of dirt and plants. At first, knowing where our lot ended made us feel safe, as if a man-made, perishable, and mortal boundary would prevent strangers from entering the space we understood as part of our home, our shelter. We use the noun *shelter* to mean *a lodging*, the verb *to shel-ter* to mean *to cover* or *take refuge*. Shelter is connected to safety. But a piece of rebar is as useless as a rib wrapped in gauze. Wes and Jim removed that stick and it became a nothing-thing, meaningless as a boundary, useless as signifier of safety. Every week they mowed into our yard, stopping at the hill so they could stare into our win-dows and watch as I built a wobbly Lego fortress with my son.

◎ ◎ ◎

Boundaries might offer a sense of safety, but they are not harmless. They are, in fact, rooted in harm. We live in a town built over the Wepawaug land of the Paugussett. On its website, a too-brief sum-mary of our city's history uses words like "settlers" and "build," "founded" and "development." More troublesome, it dubs the White settler colonists as "adventurers," just after attributing this town's current existence to a monetary transaction: "February 1, 1639, is the date the area then known as 'Wepawaug' was purchased from Ansantawae, chief sachem of the Paugusset Tribe."[8] In their work on heteropatriarchy and settler colonialism, Maile Arvin, Eve Tuck, and Angie Morrill write, "Profit is obtained by making property out of the land, as well as out of the body of the slave."[9] Harm is so often done under the guise of help, for the intention of profit. This morning, on Twitter, the poet Danez Smith writes: "Been thinking a lot about how insidiously soft the word 'settler' is when in order to 'settle' you must unsettle, disrupt, and destroy so much." How insidiously soft. The word for violent domination the same as the word for finding comfort or resolution.

◉ ◉ ◉

There is a section in Marjorie Spiegel's *The Dreaded Comparison*, where, as in *On Immunity*, as in *Brilliant Imperfection*, the relationship between healing and harm is explored. Halfway through the chapter "Vivisection," Spiegel writes of the Tuskegee syphilis experiment that began in the 1930s. White scientists thought syphilis affected White and Black people differently, and so told the men in the study—all Black and all poor—that they were being treated for their "bad blood." Even when penicillin became a routine and accepted treatment for the infection, the antibiotics that would have cured them were denied. Arvin, Tuck, and Morrill again: "The triad relationship among the industrious settler, the erased/invisibilized Native, and the ownable and murderable slave is evident in the ways in which the United States continues to exploit Indigenous, black, and other peoples deemed "illegal" (or otherwise threatening and usurping) immigrants, which is why we describe settler colonialism as a persistent structure."[10] It's been fifty years since the Tuskegee experiment was stopped. And yet. Treatment for conditions like diabetes and asthma are still often unobtainable for Americans, especially for low-income people of color, because in this country health care is catastrophically expensive and insurance is tied to employment. Even people with insurance can be devastated by medical debt when services and medications are not fully covered. Those who are supposed to heal can also be the ones who cause harm.

In this suburb, too, a history of harm and disease. There is a stretch of beach I drive past every morning on my way to take my son to school. The parking lot is frequently filled with school buses, their drivers waiting in line for coffee at the tiny takeout spot near the edge of the road. In 1776, the British dumped somewhere between 150 and 200 smallpox-infected soldiers on this shore and left them for dead.[11] Smallpox was brought here by White people, the same White people I find when I trace my own genealogy. Between 1775 and 1783, this White people's disease killed no fewer than three million Native Americans. Some hundred years later, during the epidemic of 1898, White people believed they were immune to smallpox; as it spread, they changed what they called it, using racially derogatory names instead ("N— itch," "Italian itch," "Mexican bump") to reflect the people they thought responsible for its perpetuation.[12] At the time, the vaccination carried a high risk of other infections. Despite these dangers, it was forced upon Mexican, Italian, Irish, and Black populations, sometimes at gunpoint. Weaponized. It was not until the vaccine became safer that it became common and required for all. Smallpox vaccinations of the twentieth century left a scar; my mother has one, and I have a faint memory of putting my finger over it to hide it. I was born seven years after the smallpox vaccine was determined unnecessary, the disease declared eradicated, so I am scarless.[13]

Before the vaccine, smallpox marked some survivors with facial scars, others went blind. Those living with these conditions were left behind, left out, dismissed by their communities. I return to Eli Clare: "The ableist invention of defectiveness functions as an indisputable justification not only for cure but also for many systems of oppression."[14] When a body falls outside the boundaries of our understanding of wellness, it becomes Other. In Clare's work, this ableist thinking is examined through interwoven personal narratives, his own and his friends'. He urges acceptance of what he calls his bodymind, as a trans man with cerebral palsy, and the bodyminds of others. His, theirs, are bodies not in need of fixing, but rather bodies loved and loving. Clare writes about attending a conference where he speaks about disability politics and the importance of accommodation and autonomy rather than cure and medicalization. And then, at dinner with a friend, another perspective is offered. His friend has cancer, says she does not care for the metaphor of "battle" when it comes to her illness. And yet she does not want the cancerous cells to have their way with her. Not acceptance, but something else. There is no single objective standard, he writes. Nuance requires a devotion to love.

I think there is love, too, in Kinnell's poem. After consuming part of the bear, the hunter in the poem wants to become him, so much so that he climbs inside the body. At first this feels like violence, like taking. But maybe this is a boundary-crossing love I understand. At first repulsed, it now feels a tiny bit familiar. I have imagined climbing beneath the skin of lovers when desire swells so big it extends beyond what I think my body can hold. And, when he was newly born, I stuffed my baby's tiny foot into my mouth, an indescribable urge to bite the sweetness out of it. This is not a desire to eat, nor a need to become. It is a manifestation of what it means to be all-consumed by love, a violence of love that is inexpressible in language. This is the blood of poetry.

◎ ◎ ◎

That first summer we lived here, soon after we'd finished unpacking our things on an evening close to autumn, I met June. She walked over from her house across the street, where she lives with her husband Henry and their adult son. Theirs is one of several neighborhood driveways where Wes and Jim dumped their twig piles. June and Henry's house, even older than ours, stands cool and shaded behind a couple of skinny-trunked trees. June is a retired nurse, Henry a professional musician, their son a barber. On warm evenings, when we sit on our front porch, we can hear the deep sounds of Henry's tuba practice. The day of June's first visit I was standing next to our mailbox, holding a fistful of weeds.

Pig: v. Obsolete now, but *to pig* has history as a derogatory expression of a woman giving birth, as is seen in this scrap of a letter, from 1843: "Tom told me this morning that his wife had been very ill during the night. I said, 'Has she pigged?'"

Pig has also meant to huddle, to live, or to sleep together, especially in crowded or dirty conditions. Frequently with *together*; occasionally with *in*. Also, though rare, with *along*. *To pig along* is to live in a simple, unsophisticated, or slovenly fashion. We have forgotten, or rather, we refuse to remember, that pigs are smart, emotive, compassionate. Clean, too.

A contemporary usage combines *to pig* with *out*, as in "to pig out," as in to gorge, to eat something quickly. (See also *wolf*.)

She came over to ask if anyone had yet warned us about our neighbors. *Mostly harmless. A little strange.* I told her we had met them, that they had introduced themselves. I did not say any more. I wanted her to tell me what she knew.

Henry and June have lived on this street for decades. June told me when Wes and Jim were young, they were *isolated and insular*. She said they did not get along with other kids, that they used to ring the doorbell of a girl who lived down the road, and when she answered they'd call her *Pig* and run away. She told me that Wes and Jim's father worked at the aircraft manufacturing plant in the next town, an engineer or mechanic, and one night, at dusk, Wes and Jim and their mother took all his things—clothes, shoes, tools—and threw them out onto the lawn and into the street. And then they locked the doors.

Imagine coming home from work, pulling up to the tidy yellow house where your wife and sons wait inside. You are hoping there is dinner on the stove, maybe a ballgame on the television or a deck of cards being shuffled. Imagine the sun is low enough that all is in shadows and so the lawn and the belongings strewn over it are the same shade of blue-purple. It is impossible to tell, at first, what has happened. How unfeasible it must have seemed, a hammer on the curb, underwear hanging inside-out on the trim row of hedges.

June said that Wes and Jim's father banged on the door loudly enough for all the neighbors to hear, and so they watched and listened, heard the boys and their mother screaming at him to get lost, to leave, over and over until he did. He never came back.

June told this part of the story with her own fist in the air, as if she were him, pounding on the door only to be ignored. The fear of exile is so deeply human it has become core to our culture— *Gilgamesh* and Dante's *Inferno* and Shelley's *Frankenstein* and reality television and that Taylor Swift song with Bon Iver[15]—we fear being pushed away from home. When we flipped that solitary horseshoe crab back on her feet, she seemed so grateful to return to the sea.

After she explained the details of Wes and Jim's father's ostracism, June told me that in his absence the boys became very close to their mother. *There was something weird about their closeness*, she said. She was looking at their yellow house, the railing rusty and the paint on the shingles chipped and fading. She said, *One time, when he caught me outside, Wes told me that his brother Jim and their mother were especially close. That they shared a bedroom.* My inability to react to this suburban Oedipus Rex story, a non-reaction reaction, must have made her question whether she should go on because she paused. I nodded. I could not wait to tell my husband. *He told me that they lived like husband and wife.* I can still see the way she leaned in, his confession to her becoming her confession to me as she said *without the sex part.*

Cannibalism, the consuming of one's own kind, was one of the dubious accusations Europeans used to justify their colonization of the Americas and Africa. Adams, in writing about meat, notes that colonizers failed to explain how they were able to avoid cannibalization themselves while in these countries, or how they overcame the language barriers that should have made retelling any conversations impossible. It was enough to simply accuse them and carry on. Fear of this taboo is often portrayed in stories, terror as entertainment. Giants like the one in "Jack and the Beanstalk" eat little children. In "Sing a Song of Sixpence," the four and twenty blackbirds inside the pie the king eats were, originally, four and twenty naughty boys. In the stories of Hansel and Gretel and the Baba Yaga, women cook and eat small children. Notice, though, how female cannibals cook their children, ogres and giants eat them raw. Even in this act, there is a difference of the domestic.

Piecing together the stories we heard of Wes and Jim's past with my experience living beside them calls for conjecture, a merging of personal history with neighborhood lore. The questions I asked earlier of Kinnell's hunter reemerge, slightly revised. Was their attempt to push us from our home an act of conquest or an attempt to find comfort? I see their behavior as a masculine hunger for power and dominance—terrorizing a neighborhood girl, pushing their own father away, invading our backyard space. But what if what they wanted was refuge? What if they exiled their father because *he* was a terror? Can there be healing without harm? Perhaps the rumors about their mother aren't true. Maybe there was no bed, no taboo behavior. Or maybe she was trying to protect them, comfort them.

What, then, of their gifts; the candle, the statue? If not bribes or attempts to show us they were kind, could they have been tokens of reconciliation? Attempts at connection? A hope for a rebirth of neighborliness?

If any of this is true, then what have I done? Who do I think I am? What of *my* power? Licking my own wounds as I write, passing judgments, like the final bear in Kinnell's poem, both an artist and a priest.

III. On gossip

to parrot/to slug/to swallow

AFTER DINNER, WHEN THE WEATHER ALLOWS, MATT and I walk the dog. We go the same way every time, down the street, up the hill, under the train tracks toward the center of town. On our way back home, we pass the town hall. There is a clock on the front of the cupola and a rooster-shaped weather vane on its top. The last time we walked by, I said to Matt "the time isn't right" because the clock has been broken for months. At town hall, it is forever twenty minutes past eight.

I said, "the time isn't right" and meant "the clock is wrong," but then I spent the rest of our walk thinking about how often people use that expression. The time isn't right—to have a baby, quit a job, get married, get divorced, move. "The time isn't right" is a way to say, "I am afraid to change" without having to admit to being afraid, or to say "I don't want to do that" politely. Earlier, I misremembered my favorite Barthes quote. I am sure I have referenced this fragment in front of students and colleagues and ended it incorrectly. I am ashamed, mostly because I fear that my slip will reveal I am a fraud, that I will be dismissed. I have made this molehill into a mountain. But still, like other small errors, this sneaks into my late-night thoughts and makes me cringe, and a familiar pain spreads in my chest, filling the spaces in my rib cage. I am ashamed of my small mistake because I remember the heavier consequences of larger ones.

Parrot: v. To chatter, to talk incessantly, inconsequentially, to gossip. The *OED* lists this 1701 sentence from T. Baker's *Humour of Age* (1701) as an example: "The Play-house! Ay, that's the Place where such young bold Slutts as you are nurs'd up in your Impudence; where you parrot to the Men."

To parrot insinuates a mocking, a lack of substance. There once was a parrot called Alex, who learned not only to talk in a language his handler could understand, but to communicate abstractly. There are videos of Alex on YouTube, and I am drawn to the one where he chooses between various objects: not just a green thing, or a block, but the green block. His feathers are ragged. After every question his handler asks him, Alex responds, *I wanna go back. Go back.* And maybe he meant his cage, but maybe not. He died when he was only thirty-one. (See also *ape*.)

When I confess my shames with other women—small shames like mispronouncing a word I've only read quietly to myself, or larger shames like having my credit card declined in a store—the conversation often becomes a collaborative confession. There is comradery in this sharing because these other women have had similar experiences. However, when women are talking, their conversations are sometimes dismissed as gossip—like when June told me what Wes said about his mother and his brother. *Like a marriage, without the sex part.* I told my husband. I also told other neighbors. This was not comradery.

But was it gossip? Louise Collins defines gossip's informal discourse as having "tacit norms, an etiquette, but it has no explicit formal rules governing who speaks when, the order of business..." Gossip is a conversation without restrictions. It can be impolite, fast, loud, or whispered, and allows what might otherwise be considered taboo to be discussed. "And this is why gossip," Collins continues, "with its freedoms and looseness and its value as collective and collaborative communication, is often shooed away as nothing more than idle female talk."[1] It's the female part of this type of communication that denies it its import. When I talk to other women, that talk doesn't feel idle, it feels restorative. And when June told me about Jim and Wes, I felt she was acting out of protection, her story both a warning and an explanation. If I share June's story, perhaps I will feel safer, validated. Maybe I can make others feel safer, too.

Our second summer in this house, on the night before the first day of second grade, I told my seven-year-old to put on his shoes, that we would have ice cream for dinner and then drive to the beach to watch the sunset. Our neighborhood had just been redistricted. Officials drew different lines delegating who belonged where, and so second grade meant he had to switch to another new school, his third in three years. As I opened the back door, I heard Jim and Wes's idling car muffler. I knew what came next. First, a series of slams as they brought things into their house, then intentionally loud comments about the length of our grass that would become, if we left, loud questions about where we were going, what we were doing, when we would return, and when were we planning to mow the lawn.

We tried so hard, those years Wes and Jim were our neighbors, to hide our fear from our son. When Matt and I talked about them to each other, we spoke in whispers so he wouldn't overhear. When we spoke to our child, we masked our distress, minimizing the danger while also trying to instill in him an understanding that he should stay away. *Please do not say hello to them, please do not ask them to buy anything from your school fundraiser—look! They have enough stuff. Please do not make too much noise when we're playing in the backyard, and don't let your ball roll over to their side—their lawnmower will chop it up. Please, please, please. Be careful.*

I could have shut the door, told my son never mind, we had to eat at home instead. But I'd made a promise. We had to go, even if the time wasn't right. His new red shoes were on, I was holding the door open with my hip. I had a bag on my shoulder and in it a blanket, a jug of water, and a fistful of napkins. I held my phone in one hand, my keys in the other. We walked out of the house, into the driveway, and got into the car. When I closed the rear passenger door, though, Wes heard. He stepped out of their garage with his hands in the air. Without waving back, I got in the car and pulled away.

The ice cream shop has a pink roof. They offer flavors for humans and for dogs. We ordered chocolate ice cream with thick chunks of brownie, our sugar cones tipped over into paper bowls to catch the drips. We ate on a bench, our faces and hands still a little sticky when we got back into the car to head to the beach. There, the sand was warm, as was the air, though there was a snap to the breeze. If we talked about anything more than school and hermit crabs I don't remember. We left without putting our shoes back on, under a bruise-purple dusk the same color as the inside of an oyster shell.

Jim and Wes's car was still in the driveway when we pulled in. They were standing on their lawn, rearranging the solar-powered lights lining their sidewalk, their side of the driveway, and the perimeter of their house. Because it wasn't all the way dark, the lights flickered each time they were moved.

I pulled into our driveway, turned off the car, gathered our things. Trying so hard to keep my voice calm, I told my child we had to be quick about getting into the house. I reached around to unlatch his seatbelt. Then I heard a damp bump on my window, loud as the smack of rotted fruit. Wes had his hand pressed against the glass, hard enough that his flattened fingers appeared yellow and bloodless. His chin jutted out, the gray wave of his hair a frizzled corona beneath his hat. Stubble shadowed his cheeks and as he yelled, spit caught in the corners of his mouth. I did not scream because my child still sat in the back trying to shake the sand off his feet.

Rude. Rude. The volume of Wes's repetitive accusation fell somewhere between conversation and yell. On their side of the driveway, leaning over the hood of their car, Jim stood shaking his head, then said *And all this time, I thought you were a good girl.* Wes's hand stayed pressed against my car window. All the heat in my body rushed toward my belly, my softest spot became the warmest.

When someone waves to you, you wave back. You say Hello. *You acknowledge them,* he said, the word *acknowledge* stretched thin as his lips. He yelled in bobs and weaves, the word *rude* reappearing and then darting forward to point out that my poor manners meant I was a poor mother. *What kind of example are you setting for your son when you ignore me? How dare you ignore me? Your child is watching. You are supposed to wave back.* My son and I sat silent in our seats, safe, but precariously close to unsafe, like two Jonahs in a whale.

⊚ ⊚ ⊚

In *Guidebook to Relative Strangers*, Camille Dungy occasionally writes to her daughter directly. She writes to her of love, messy and unwieldly, and also of unfathomable loss. These two feelings are essential to the experience of motherhood; a tug of war between *I love you so much I would die for you*, and *I am certain I would die without you*. Early into the book, as she writes to her infant daughter, she also writes about a ship called the *Brooklyn*. In 1846, over two hundred Mormons, many of them young mothers with children, climbed on board to search for a new home in California. They were blown off course and many died. Dungy lists the names of the mothers and children lost, and those other mothers who survived the journey, sick and exhausted and surely teetering between grief and hope. She writes at the end of this chapter, "I don't know if there is a name for this in any language. This hope and hurt and hunger I hold when I hold you." I remember this night of Wes, that my son's hand was still small enough to be covered by mine. I remember thinking, *I would kill for you*.

Even in the midst of knowing that what Wes was shouting was unfounded, untrue, and unwarranted—the irony of his hand against my car, shouting about *my* rudeness—I wondered, What kind of example *was* I setting? Had I been unmannered? Would it have been smarter just to wave? Should I be braver, now, in this moment? What would that look like? A flung door, a scream, a kick? In the preface to his essay collection *Wild Things: The Disorder of Desire*, Jack Halberstam writes of the wild/civilized opposition. "...we must find a way around the treacherous binary logics that set the wild in opposition to the modern, the *civilized*, the cultivated, and the real."[2] We use the term *civilized* often as a synonym for well-mannered, wild as another word for uncouth. This duality is both about nature and the control of it. Those "civilized" manners are drenched in white supremacy, heteronormative gender roles, and class. It comes as no surprise, then, that a lack of manners is linked with animal behavior, a way for the white heteropatriarchy to Other anyone outside of that space. Aligning *wild* with *animal* is a shortcut to dehumanization, a practice that stretches back centuries, and often begins in childhood. The very concept of wilderness is an invention by White people.[3] Here is what Erasmus of Rotterdam wrote in a handbook of manners for children in the sixteenth century: "Some people, no sooner than they have sat down, immediately stick their hands into the dishes of food. This is the manner of wolves."[4] Wes accused me of being rude as he shouted, spit, and slammed his body against my car.

The weaponization of politeness is certainly not limited to White men and is often a tool used by White women. Looking specifically at White southern female students in her classroom, Sabrina N. Ross writes of politeness used as a weapon. A Black woman teaching young White women about social justice in education, Ross initially read the silence in her classroom as politeness. But when she reconsidered their silence alongside notes from her student evaluations, it became apparent that her students used white silence as a form of psychological violence. By staying quiet, they were dismissing Ross altogether, as if she wasn't their teacher, as if she wasn't even in the room. Like second-wave feminism, civilized manners are focused on the White middle class. When White people make the rules, they also get to determine who breaks them. "'I just know you're a good man,'" said the Grandmother to The Misfit in Flannery O'Connor's "A Good Man is Hard to Find," just after his two henchmen took her son into the woods to shoot him. "'You're not a bit common!'"

As Wes continued to yell about my misbehavior, I stayed in my seat, quiet as a cabbage. Did I choose silence to be polite or was I just afraid? Wes continued to rant, his hand pressed to my window, for several minutes before he paused to catch his breath. I tried to open the door. *Wes*, I said, *you need to let us out.* He pushed his hand harder against the window. *I will call the police. I will call them right now.* As I pulled the door handle, he pushed his other hand against the window, his brute force against mine. If I could have opened the door, I am unsure whether I would have bolted toward the house or punched him in the jaw.

Slug: v. To punch. But also, and perhaps more closely aligned to the animal itself, to move idly, lazily, slowly. Or, to be lazy or slow. Or, to hinder or delay.

To load a gun with slugs is called slugging, though a bullet moves at about 1,700 miles per hour.

To slug it out means to fight it out.

To drug or exploit, like by slipping something into someone's drink in a bar, is called slugging. Additionally, to drink quickly, especially beer, is known as slugging.

A slug is like a snail without a shell. It is completely vulnerable to the world.

But I couldn't get out. I imagined, briefly, what it would be like to drive backward, run him over, pull up and do it again. If I could get out of the car I could jab my keys into his eyes, grab the trash bin and throw it, take him out at the knees. But I was stuck.

◎ ◎ ◎

We looked at three other houses before we bought this one. One was too big and needed renovations we could not afford. One had a kitchen too small for two people to be in at once. The bathroom door in the third house couldn't close all the way if a tall person sat on the toilet. How perfect this house seemed to us then. Just right. Of course I did not hit Wes in my driveway. After he screamed himself satisfied, he dropped his hand from my window and I was able to leave the car. I grabbed our bag, told my wide-eyed child to head straight into the house. I did not smash Wes's fingers in my door, but I wished our dog was vicious. From inside I could still hear Wes repeating and circling his assertions that I was a bad mother, a rude person, that I should be ashamed of myself. (I was ashamed of myself. But not for ignoring him. My shame was darker, deeper, though I could not name it then.) I locked and bolted the doors, shut the windows, pulled the curtains closed. It was time to prepare for the first day of school. I followed my son upstairs, started the shower for him. Then I called Matt at work, fear in my throat like vomit.

Swallow: v. To bring into the stomach through the throat or gullet. The opposite of to spit.

Figuratively, *to swallow* is used as a verb to describe ways things disappear. (See also *squirrel*.) To swallow one's spittle is to suppress one's anger, to swallow the anchor is to quit sailing. A swallow is a bird so aerodynamic it hunts on the wing. (See also *hawk*.) So many versions of consuming.

My husband is an artist, too. He draws as he works, watches TV, or talks on the phone. At night, he draws while I write this.

Drawing, for him, is almost a compulsion and is compulsory to his thinking-through. When he draws, he draws cartoons, some animals but mostly people, whole pages of faces and heads. He redraws the same face the same way I will rewrite the same idea in a dozen different ways. Recently I was reading an interview with the artists Dani and Sheilah ReStack, and Sheilah mentioned fragmentation as a way to deal with conflict.[5] She was talking about balancing art and family, but I can't help but see Matt's drawings now as representational of our disembodied feelings, so many of his faces twisted in anger or disgust, reminiscent of what had once been hurled at us, and filled us.

Once my son was safe, in the shower and out of earshot, I called Matt at work even though I knew he was powerless to help me. He was two and a half hours south of us, a train and two subway rides away. He couldn't just come home and confront Wes or comfort us, but a phone call is a connection of voices when bodies are far apart. I called to commiserate and collaborate, and also because it felt important he know what had happened as soon as possible, just in case Wes wasn't through with his rant, just in case something worse happened. I imagined Matt sketching faces on a new sheet of paper as he suggested he call the police from his office. The last time I'd called, the officer who came to take my statement told me it was "just a neighbor altercation." The *just* dismisses their actions as *only*, as *merely*. The threat of a bigger violence felt like worms writhing beneath my skin as I replayed the evening over the phone, pacing in our bedroom. I hung up so he could make the call. Then I went into the bathroom, told my son it was time to get out of the shower. I grabbed his towel from the hook, wrapped him up so tightly he complained it hurt.

◎ ◎ ◎

It became a habit, whenever I saw June, to tell her what was happening with the brothers. I saw these quick talks as a means to keep her posted, but also to open the door for her to share with me more of their history. I needed to know everything about what they had done before to collect evidence about what we were up against. These edge-of-the-street confessions may have looked like mere neighbor-gossip, but were actually where we released our private thoughts into the air of the public. Our friendship formed a trinity of validation, protection, and commiseration.

Though "gossip" might be shorthand for "women talking," and though women talking to each other can be restorative, protective, or friendly, it can also be, as Ross points out, weaponized. This weaponization has a long history.

In the mid-eighteenth century, in Barnstable, Massachusetts, where some of my White family lived and still lives, an enslaved woman named Nanny became pregnant. The White people in town insisted on knowing who the father was, and over the course of her pregnancy Nanny named two different men, both White: John Otis, the son of a wealthy lawyer and David Manning, an indentured servant. The town began speculating, swapping gossip and theories about paternity.

In a court system committed to protecting the rights of White men, and at a time when people believed pregnancy was only possible if the woman orgasms and impossible in cases of rape, Nanny first explained that she'd had sex with Otis and that when it was over, he gave her money. However, she did not say he was the baby's father. She also didn't say whether her encounter was consensual or rape because "She had little ability to reject the advances of a white man or claim that the sex was forced."[6]

The relationship she described with Manning was different, though similarly restrained. She explained the locations where they had sex, listed where she may have been impregnated. But because her sexuality was policed and she could be punished, she withheld details about pain or pleasure, though the implication of pleasure existed in the mere fact that she was pregnant.

Even if she had explicitly said she was raped, even if she formally charged one of the men, the charge would likely not hold. Although the White townspeople insisted on her revealing the father's identity, it also asserted her personhood, and pushed back on the idea that enslaved people should stay quiet.

It is unclear exactly why Nanny told the members of the court both stories. Maybe she wanted her truth to go on record even if it meant pairing it with a lie. Perhaps she knew that even if Otis was the father, she had a greater chance of successfully accusing a lower-status man of paternity, that it was more believable that a poor man had sex with an enslaved woman than one of high social status. Perhaps she was protecting her unborn baby, knowing if someone was required to pay child support, her baby was less likely to be sold.

Maybe she was trying to keep herself alive, as documents show that her enslavers pushed for her to pin paternity on Otis, either hoping for greater financial support, or trying to gain leverage in the ongoing feud between themselves and the wealthy Otis family.

In the end she said it was the poorer man. Manning was angry, though when he stormed to Nanny's, her mother, also enslaved, told him she had no choice; Otis was just too powerful. She told him no one would ever believe her anyway, had actually never believed her, and had used their power and influence to elicit from her the answers they wanted to hear.

However, even with paternity named, Nanny's life and body were still a source for White people's gossip and violence. Months later, when she went into labor, she was interrogated again. The women in town still were not convinced Nanny was telling the truth. In the birthing room, midwives (who were also called gossips) threatened she'd be "whipped, hanged, and damned" if she didn't reveal the truth about her baby's father. They believed the pain of labor and its proximity to death meant women would tell the truth, and these birth-confessions carried a lot of weight in town gossip spaces.

The women attending Nanny's labor included David Manning's family. They, along with Nanny's mother, of course wanted Nanny to recant and name Otis. But Nanny held her ground. In fact, exhausted but nearing delivery, she testified that Otis never touched her, that Manning had actually given her the money, and that he had claimed to be Otis in order to trick her. With this new confession, any lingering uncertainty disappeared. She had only had sex with Manning, so he alone could be the father.

The White women were furious. They wanted to protect the reputations of the White boys they knew.[7] After Nanny gave birth, afraid others would believe the words of an enslaved Black woman over their own, those White women committed themselves to secrecy. Then the gossip that had swarmed Barnstable for months was used in the Otis family's defamation suit.

Emily Jeannine Clark writes, "Nanny's story demonstrates how gossip, rather than the courts, could be used as a tool of social control—even if the wealthy man went unpunished, the whispering would damage his reputation. Gossip, a social currency, could cause real damage."[8] But it could not wholly validate or vindicate Nanny. After the trial (a trial that was, remember, about preserving the reputations of White men) records about Nanny fade, hinting that perhaps she was sold. There is no record of what happened to her baby.[9]

◎ ◎ ◎

Gossip is powerful, though often considered taboo and brushed away as frivolous or meritless. Historically, gossip was feared by slaveholders who tried to keep enslaved people from talking to each other, aware of the power in whispers. More recently, women have created Facebook groups and Reddit threads warning other women about dangerous men. Canada, Australia, and the UK have Clare's Law, which allows people to apply for information on partners they suspect might have histories of abuse. Sex offender registry lists are available to the public in the US. Gossip is shared knowledge among people whose voices are not heard by those with power. But in this tradition of shared stories, we find a history of discreditation—no help without harm. Maria Tatar writes, "The idea of loose talk spills over into the concept of loose morals, reminding us that the verbal and sexual freedom of women creates high anxiety and incites efforts to contain and police their liberties and especially any libertine behaviors."[10] The policing of language, like the policing of bodies, is a form of control.

And though used maliciously at times, gossip remains a source of protection, a means of storytelling and archive. This gossip-as-narrative-making, as Tatar also explains, is what folklorists and anthropologists have noted is the root of story. "A made-up story might have its origins in the real-life account of, say, a woman's dread of marriage or of another woman's resentment of a stepchild, but it will also disguise those accounts by depersonalizing their content, projecting them into an imaginary world, and exaggerating and enlarging their stakes."[11] It is a personal story turned outward to relate to others outside of oneself, to be handed down as a lesson for readers to learn from.[12]

◎ ◎ ◎

Here's a story:

Once upon a time there was a family. A mother, a stepfather, and a little boy. The family moved to an old white house in a suburb near the sea. Next door to the family lived two brothers, strange strangers who wandered the streets, dropping trash and sticks wherever they went. The brothers wanted to push the family far, far away so they could live in the old white house themselves, so they played tricks on the family. One day the mother took her boy out for ice cream and the day was so beautiful she forgot to be afraid. When they returned home, she didn't notice the shadow coming around the driveway until the taller, meaner brother trapped her and her little boy in the car with his big hands. It was then when she realized how much stronger he was, how wild his eyes were, and she pulled and she pulled on the door to keep her little boy safe.

But how does it end?

◎ ◎ ◎

Even after we went inside, Jim and Wes still shouted in the driveway, just below my son's window. I got him out of the shower and helped him get ready for bed, then I told him he didn't have to sleep in his room. Instead, I set up a cot in our room, next to our bed. As I put a clean pillowcase on his pillow, I realized that what I was doing was maybe not all that different from what June had told me about Wes and Jim's mom.

The police finally called back. I whispered to them not to come, told them my little boy was nearly asleep, that tomorrow was the first day of school and he was already so nervous. I did not say, *What are you going to do that I haven't already done?* Instead, I said, *The time isn't right for you to come.* I hung up, checked the doors again, then climbed up into the attic to keep watch.

In the story of Little Red Riding Hood, the wolf eats the grandmother and her granddaughter, but they are saved by a woodsman who cuts them out of the wolf's body with a pair of scissors, a rescue via cesarean rebirth. When the darkness fully settled and it was clear I would not be coming back outside, Wes and Jim drove away.

The huntsmen in the red riding hood story didn't just cut the wolf open with his scissors, but he replaced their weight in his stomach with stones. I left the attic, laid on our bed and watched my son sleep. Gently, I touched his wet hair.

IV. On performance

to cow/to cock/to clam

THREE OR FOUR TIMES A WEEK WHILE IN GRADUATE school, I took one train from our city into Stamford, where I transferred to a second train that took me to the Bronx. I passed the twenty-minute wait between by wearing headphones to block out the noise so I could study. In those days, I was exhausted by the commute from place to place and from student to motherhood, and so any time I could find to catch up on reading I took.

Usually, when the train arrived, I got in and walked from car to car, making my way toward the front to find a seat near a window, holding my breath in the open air of the in-between where one wrong step would mean slipping off and under the train's wheels. But this day, before I found a seat, the conductor tapped me on the shoulder. I took off my headphones and reached for my ticket, assuming he was in a rush maybe, or thought I had boarded the wrong train. But he didn't want my ticket. The conductors here wear stiff blue shirts, official hats, and sensible shoes. He asked, *Did you see that guy? Do you know him?* while pointing outside at an older man in a long tan coat. *That guy? No.* The officialness of his uniform made me read his concern as scolding while he told me the man had followed me onto the train. This conductor noticed that I wasn't paying attention—the headphones, the open book—and that the man was following me too closely. He stopped him. When he found him ticketless, he made him leave. I listened to the conductor, red-faced with shame because I should have known better, and then I thanked him. He told me to pay more attention. I promised to be more aware, sat down in a rear-facing seat and backed my way into the city.

◎ ◎ ◎

My last semester of graduate school, I struggled to decide what to write my thesis on. I was torn between two different ideas: the children (or lack thereof) in American Naturalist novels written between 1850 and 1880, and the intersection of performance art and narrative forms of memoir. I was thirty-four, thirty-five, thirty-six, and both a mother and a student. These two ideas seemed to be manifestations of my two selves. Many of my colleagues seemed put off by my motherhood. I spent much of my time pretending to know what I was doing.

I abandoned the novels study and focused wholly on studying performance art, drawn to women who used gesture to compensate for and supplement verbal and written language. Here is an art composed of bodily utterances. Performance confronts audiences in ways written works cannot, often because they take up space in ways books don't. Performance has the potential to make body art from body tragedy, an act I see as a kind of anti-shame. *Look at me!* an artist says, *And think about what you see!* When the man followed me across the platform and onto that train, I might have been listening to interviews with performance artists. I might have been reading about Emma Sulkowicz, the Columbia student who was, at that time, carrying the mattress she was allegedly sexually assaulted on. I wanted to place her work within a canon of other female artists' work that simultaneously embodies and disembodies the alienation of female experience. Her "Carry that Weight" project seemed to me to be a subversion of the public's inevitable accusatory gaze by confronting its inevitability head-on, a deconstruction of expectations. That which can disrupt can also cohere.

◎ ◎ ◎

In her 1974 performance *Rhythm 0*, Marina Abramović set a table with seventy-two objects—a rose, perfume, scissors, a gun—and labeled herself as an object as well. Then she stood silently as those in the gallery started, gently at first, to give her objects, and then stopped being gentle and moved toward violence. They cut her clothes, sexually assaulted her, wrote on her skin, all before someone put a bullet into the gun and placed the gun in her hand. In a short retrospective video about this performance, Abramović explains her purpose for this piece: "I want[ed] to know what the public's about."

It seems to me the public has not so much a tendency toward violence, but a propensity for escalation when the opportunity presents itself. Even without an art exhibit, we decide whether to inflict pleasure or pain on each other every day. We decide whether to drive straight into traffic or hold open a door. We decide whether to follow someone onto a train car. Usually, we do not break the unspoken social contracts of space, safety, and autonomy. We merge, hold doors, stand clear. The escalation toward violence tips the second we stop seeing each other as people. After six hours, Abramović began to move, stopping the exhibit. When she did, everyone ran away. She went back to her hotel room, where she found she had "a big piece of white hair" where there hadn't been white hair before, her body's instant reaction to what happened. Wes had trapped me in my car, but long before that, they'd given us a candle. They escalated their antics from there. I will never know what their tipping point was, but I think it happened long before we moved in.

◎ ◎ ◎

In the still photos I have seen of this exhibit, Abramović's face is blank; her skin pallid, eyes distant in a look of resigned recognition. It is a look that seems to acknowledge humanity's potential for violence. A hand will always be ready to reach for the gun that will always exist. Who was the person who loaded and then put it in her hand? In Frazer Ward's *No Innocent Bystanders: Performance Art and Audience*, he claims what is so disturbing about *Rhythm 0* is that it asks the question: "If my body is not mine (if it is not me), if it is not my property, whose is it?"[1] In Akron, Ohio 1851, Sojourner Truth repeated, "Ain't I a woman?"[2] But in 1945, Barthes's Swiss physicians, post-rib removal, presented him with his bone fragment. The assertion: *my body belongs to me*. In June 2022, Roe v. Wade was overturned in America. Perhaps it is already obvious, but bodily autonomy is most often for men.

◎ ◎ ◎

I should have been more vigilant on the train platform. Before this happened, shortly before we moved into our house, Wes followed Matt on his morning train commute.

Cow. v. "To depress with fear" (Johnson); to dispirit, overawe, intimidate.

Matt noticed Wes at the station, which was odd, but not alarming. Not yet. The station is a short walk from where we live. Wes paced up and down the platform, talking on his phone. When the train arrived and everyone boarded, Wes sat across the aisle and behind Matt, a stealthy move that put him far enough away to be out of sight but still within earshot.

Matt also likes to make his way to the front of the train once it nears the terminal. A position near the door makes it easier to exit the train and catch the shuttle across town, where another subway carries him underground like a mole in a pneumatic bank tube, further south to the office. When he left his seat, Wes did the same, following behind with his finger in one ear, his phone still pressed against his face.

They seem nice, he said. *They live over on R——. They only got the house because the old owners don't like us. But we met them and they seem nice. When they were at the house for the inspection, we watched from our garage. We offered Jerry cash but he didn't want to sell to us. I went to where they used to live once but no one was home. I talked to their landscaper. He said they're good people.*

Matt recalled this conversation to me over the phone once he got to his office. Whenever he calls instead of sending a text, I assume something is terribly wrong. We didn't have a landscaper, but Matt did have a neighbor called Eddie who liked to check the depth of the stream in Matt's backyard. Eddie carried treats in his pocket for the neighborhood dogs, let his cat drape herself around his neck. He couldn't have known that Wes wanted anything more than friendly banter.

I listened without commenting as Matt told me how Wes talked on his phone until the train stopped, how then he got out and quickly became swallowed up in the chaos of busy people going places. There is no reason to wonder who was on the other end of the call. There has never been any phone service in the tunnel.

◉ ◉ ◉

Last night, like many nights, I peppered my husband with questions, making sure my memory here was right.[3] Sitting side by side on our couch, I asked whether he'd thought about confronting Wes. He said he was too stunned to say anything, too caught off-guard. Then I asked him, as he carried on with his normal routine, if he felt scared or ashamed. *Ashamed, no. It was weird, but nothing more.* I must have thought the same, back then, and dismissed the whole interaction as odd but not something to worry over. We still moved in, hadn't we? And besides, had Wes even done anything wrong?

Cock: v. To fight, wrangle, do battle. To behave boastfully, to swagger and strut, to brag, or crow over. (See also *crow*, also *swan*.)

    This is an old word. Old as sunrises. In the fourteenth century, hay was cocked into conical heaps.

    The use of cock as a synonym for *swagger* first appears in the sixteenth century. By the seventeenth century, it was used as coarse slang: to cock was to have sex.

    In addition, to cock means to cause (especially a part of the body) to stick up in an assertive or jaunty way. To cock your head. This usage first appeared in the seventeenth century, so we've been cocking our heads and our hats for almost 400 years. We've been cocking guns since 1598. (To *cock about*, also called *dick about*, means to annoy a person or waste a person's time. See also *badger*.)

When I take what my husband said and add his version to mine, then write it down here, I am reinventing an un-fun version of the telephone game we played as children. Stories passed and meanings made; a gossip game, mouth to ear.

◉ ◉ ◉

Theresa Hak Kyung Cha's performance piece *Mouth to Mouth* is an eight-minute recording of her mouth, up close, as she lips eight Korean vowels in a "meditation on how language can express nuanced feelings of displacement."[4] Her staticky mouth, like a bad phone connection, sounds as much like rain as it does old televisions. As the picture fades in and out, the static looks like a puddle, her mouth looks like a drain, a fish, a cave, a silent scream, a song. There is a bright glint on the teeth in her near-smile.

Looking at a mouth that close disorients the looker. It destabilizes because you know her mouth is hers, but zoomed in, it could be someone, or something, else. Cha's mouth is her mouth but, as those vowel sounds are visible but unable to be heard, also the mouth of Korean American women who have been dismissed, silenced, or ignored because of their language. Ryan Claycomb unpacks this aspect of performance art when he explains "...individual monologic performances are significant both as solo pieces of self-representation and as part of a collective of voices that challenge the uniformity of a patriarchal norm."[5] Her mouth, a mouth, up close is a confrontation with the overlap of sex, sustenance, and language. (How many ways can a woman be consumed?)

Cathy Park Hong writes of Cha's life and art, and about how very little was written about her brutal death in 1982. Cha was attacked by Joseph Sanza, a man who was a stranger to the other women he raped (but did not murder), but whom Cha knew. He was the security guard at the building where her husband worked, which is where she was going and where she was raped and killed. She knew him, and therefore could identify him had he let her go.

He killed her to keep her quiet. To shut her mouth. Even when her murder is mentioned, the fact that she was raped first isn't, a fact Hong calls "an omission so stubborn I had to consult court records to confirm that she was also sexually assaulted."[6] In *Mouth to Mouth*, there are stretches where the static sounds give way to water and bird sounds, so that nature's song seems to come out of her mouth. This feels to me, in hindsight, like a gift, a hope or a reminder that when we think we perceive silence, sometimes we might still hear the birds.

The erasure of Sanza's violence against Cha is a small part of an historical and systemic silencing. During Japanese rule, the Korean people were forced to give up their names and language. In the coverage that does exist about Cha's death, they call her only an "Oriental Jane Doe." Forty years after her death, here in the US there is an increase in Asian American hate crimes after Trump calls COVID the "China virus." Toward the end of her piece on Cha, Hong asks, "But where does the silence that neglects her end, and where does the silence that respects her begin?"[7]

Cha's work draws attention to the silencing of language, but also to its visceralness as she juxtaposes static and silence with the wet openness of her mouth. Often, performance art, especially in pieces created by female artists, pushes back against silencing. Or, as in Abramović's, draws attention to it. Sulkowicz, too, was resisting the silencing of her alleged attack, her loudness came from taking up space. Performance art is anti-silence, polyphonic as it communicates through the visual, physical, and aural.

◎ ◎ ◎

Because Wes's fake phone call act on the train was one of the first times either brother had been so overtly strange, but still not overtly violent—still, perhaps, polite—we did not know how to interpret his actions.[8] Wes's performance was one of loud power, an act that drew attention to himself as a person of stature, a dominant force we could not ignore. He wanted to be heard. His voice, he knew, wielded power. The station platform and then the train itself transformed into a stage for a show that, unlike an act of intentional performance art, wasn't aimed at drawing attention to misplaced power; but, because of the power already inherent in his maleness, rather solidified the patriarchal domination he'd already acquired.

◎ ◎ ◎

It wasn't long after we moved in that the two brothers firmly asserted their intent to push us out of our home, to dominate this part of the neighborhood. In the first few months we lived here, they mowed our lawn, peered into our windows, yelled at me and at my mother, used my middle name in the driveway as a way of letting me know they had looked me up, paced the sidewalk, stood in front of our windows, and followed me in my car. On a Saturday shortly after we'd moved in, I overheard Matt on the phone with a friend on the West Coast. Eavesdropping, I heard him recount to his friend the day Wes followed him on the train and then describe all the disconcerting encounters we'd had. My husband may not have felt fear or shame about what was happening to us, but with each encounter stacked on another, I felt a crisp-edged anger and humiliation. I hadn't told many friends what we were living with, a part of me needing to ignore it, another part worried what I felt would be seen as hysteria, an exaggeration. As Matt talked, I felt an increasing desire to stop him, to silence him, the redness crawling over my skin like when my mother would sit at the kitchen table, phone cord stretched from the wall as she coiled it around her finger, telling my grandmother every private moment of my day, two disembodied voices meeting through stretches of telephone wire.

◎ ◎ ◎

In Eula Biss's essay "Time and Distance Overcome," she traces the history of telephone poles. First, telephones were playthings of the rich. Then they became more common, and the poles were seen as a blight on neighborhoods, so people threatened the telephone workers and cut down the poles. "The War on Telephone Poles was fueled, in part, by that terribly American concern for private property and a reluctance to surrender it to a shared utility,"[9] she writes.

Then, White Americans found a different use for telephone poles. Lynching. (Another American invention.) "The poles, of course, were not to blame. It was only coincidence that they became convenient as gallows, because they were tall and straight, with a crossbar, and because they stood in public places. And it was only coincidence that the telephone pole so closely resembled a crucifix."[10] Objects become weapons when people are no longer seen as such. I am no longer surprised by the limitlessness of human cruelty, or by the ways White people innovate their power into violence.

◉ ◉ ◉

At a Christmas party at June and Henry's our first December here, we met a couple from farther up the road. They, too, had a history of being harassed by the brothers. At this party, they told us that Jim worked for the phone company. They told us they thought he listened in on their calls. *How do you know?* I asked them. *Once,* said the man whose name I no longer remember, *he asked us how our visit home to England was.* They had never told him they were traveling. Is it possible that Jim had merely overheard them talking to someone else? Is it even possible for him to tap into a phoneline? When does hypothesis become paranoia? When Matt hung up the phone, I asked him not to talk about the brothers anymore. Paranoia or protection, I don't know, but it wasn't long after that we decided to disconnect our landline.

Clam: v. Though obsolete now, to clam once meant to smear, daub, or spread unctuous matter on or with. Throughout its history, the verb form of clam is linked with its animal form: slimy and sticky, moist and gelatinous.

To bedaub a thing so that it sticks is to clam that thing together.

To clam up is to clamp a mouth shut, to be silent. It has also meant to clutch, grasp, or grope, because a clam is like a barnacle. Then, of course, it has always meant the act of catching the animals themselves. As in, *They went clamming at the beach*. A linguistic move as grotesque as it is efficient. (See also *fish*, also *badger*.)

After Emma Sulkowicz carried her mattress through Manhattan, she performed a follow up show in LA and I went.[11] I went to bear witness and to record what I saw for my research, but instead I became part of her show. In a small gallery in Chinatown, she displayed a mannequin version of herself—an un-her holding an iPad preloaded with common questions and answers about her mattress project. This doppelgänger version spoke for her and in so doing, allowed her to refrain from repeating herself while still setting the record straight. The real Sulkowicz was there, too, sitting on a platform next to the mannequin her, still and quiet in a patch of sun. There was no one else there when I arrived. Walking alone through the space felt voyeuristic, but that was the point. When

I sat in front of her, I didn't know what to say. For a moment, I thought I would tell her about the brothers, tell her what I knew about being followed and looked at, judged by strangers. Maybe it was the Los Angeles sunlight or maybe it was the jet lag or the funny way I'd slept, but I felt pulled to tell her, a stranger, about the brothers, the opposite of what I'd wanted my husband to do with his friend. Instead, I told her only about my thesis. I don't think this avoidance was a shirking of secrets, because this confession of my interest in her work also seemed intimate. I could not talk about what didn't feel real.

We exchanged email addresses, but we never made contact again. I felt embarrassed, the only one there, in the space of a gallery with someone I had studied closely but did not know at all. The uncanniness of her object-self felt too close to our real-selves. Besides, the moment seemed better frozen in time. We do not owe each other anything more than the shared space. An end to that small part of the performance, for her and for me.

◎ ◎ ◎

What might have happened had the conductor not stopped the stranger? How might he have escalated our interaction? He could have followed me onto the train. And then what? Unwanted conversation? An unwanted touch? A push in the split second of air as I changed cars? A weapon can be a hand, a mouth, a blade, a gun. He could have reached into my backpack. But for what? A squashed sandwich? A just-through-the-wash dollar bill? What if I had seen him coming? What then? Run up the downward-moving escalator? Push *him* onto the tracks? Scream? If I screamed would everyone stop, or would no one bother to hear?

What might have happened if I had confronted Wes and Jim in our driveway? Taking up space is dangerous. Relinquishing it is, too.

Performance art messes with time. It is ephemeral but can be archived if recorded or written about. Necessary and urgent even when, like in Cha's piece, it is languid. A forcing of attention in order to focus attention somewhere it usually isn't. Years after *Rhythm 0*, Abramović was reenacting a different show, *Thomas' Lips*, at the Guggenheim. In this exhibit, she repeatedly carves a five-point star into her belly with a razor blade. After she cut herself several times, a young woman in the audience shouted, crying, "You can stop. You don't have to do this." She was immediately answered by a man in the audience who responded, "Yes she does."[12]

V. On catching and being caught

to dog/to bat/to fly/to peacock/to gander/to squirrel

SOMETIME IN LATE AUTUMN 2014, I WENT TO THE police station and walked up to the plexiglass window that separates the officers from the civilians. The tall White man with a buzz cut who came out to talk to me was dismissive. *What do you want us to do, ma'am?* I wanted a restraining order. Unless our neighbors were caught in the act of trespassing, unless we could prove without a doubt that we were being followed, there wasn't anything they would do. "The law meted out by cops is the law created by men,"[1] Virginie Despentes writes. I left the station angry and went straight home. In the driveway, I wondered if we should move.

I did not call the police every time Wes and Jim were in the yard, in our driveway, in our trash. But I did call them several times, more than a few. Since police only arrive after a crime occurs, they were never caught.[2]

If I needed evidence to get official protection, then I was willing to try, even if there was part of me that understood a piece of paper was only that. I knew enough stories of violence to know that if I did not try and something happened, I would be to blame.

We bought a security camera, even though we were wary about surveillance, both as a practice and as an expense. It came with complicated directions and endless lengths of wire. I drilled holes through the exterior walls of our house and through the hardwood floors and then Matt threaded the wires through those holes and into a recording device that connected to our television. There was an app that allowed us to log in and watch from our phones.

Dog: v. To follow at the heels of, to track (a person, or their trail, footsteps, etc.) closely and persistently. As is seen in *Twelfth Night*: "I haue dogg'd him like his murtherer." How close murderer is to mother.

There is an obsolete usage, from the early 1600s, where *to dog* meant *to haunt*. An invisible threat. More recently, it is used to mean to shirk, or to avoid. But *to dog* can also imply one is being a persistent source of distress to someone.

We also say, "to hound."

The daily anticipation of their presence had, up until we put the camera in, felt like a gloved hand around my neck. With it installed, a different kind of anticipation set in. No longer a choking, itching dread, instead, I wanted them to pull up. I wanted them to see what we had done, to know what we were prepared to do. I wanted to record them and then bring the footage down to the poorly lit police station, show our proof to the dismissive cop, be granted the restraining order. Fear transformed to vengeance masks itself as relief.

I no longer remember how many days passed before Jim and Wes appeared. It could not have been long. It never was. I do know the camera was visible from where they parked their car, no branches or shrubs hiding its location, its lens pointed directly at where they stood. The wariness I'd always held about surveillance, its power and invasiveness, disappeared. How far would I go to stop them? On their side of the driveway, they opened their car doors and then slammed them, opened and then slammed again.

It was fall, but not yet cold. The windows were open. I turned on our television as soon as I heard them pull in. And then there they were, standing side by side on the TV screen in our living room, their images grainy and over-exposed. For several minutes they only stared up at it, their heads tilted, Jim's mouth slightly open, Wes's tightly shut, until he began repeating, *We see your camera. We see it. I see what you did.* They turned back to their car, resumed opening and closing the doors, and then stopped. Facing the camera again with their fingers pointing toward it, Wes said, *You can't fool us. Joke's on you. Joke's on you. You're not going to catch us.*

To say the joke is on me implies I am trying to make them look foolish but am only succeeding in being foolish myself. To say I cannot catch them means there must be something that can be caught. One of these feels truer than the other.

Their yelling entered through our living room window and took up all the air in the room. Since the camera only recorded image, I felt I was watching a terrible movie with surround sound, their voices not coming out of the television, but through the windows, bouncing off the plaster walls. How long did they yell before Matt, who was at the grocery store or the home improvement store or out helping his parents, came home? How strange, to see our car cut through the scene on the TV. If it had been me coming home to see them standing next to each other in the driveway, their sil-houette shaped like an open pair of scissors, I would have driven past. But Matt parked, got out of the car. Wes walked toward him with loping steps. Finger in my husband's face, he spit as he yelled. *You can't fool me.* I didn't want to watch them anymore. I could not stop watching them. *I know you have a crush on me. You want to watch me. You want to look at me. I know it.*

Bat: v. To hit away, to strike or hit a ball with a bat. There is also the US expression *to bat the eyes*, which is a fluttering of eyelashes seen as a way of flirting. *To bat*, then, can be an act of violence or an act of sex.

I'd almost forgotten this conversation in the driveway had happened. Much of what Wes said to us was baffling, so specifics become blurry. Untangling the knot of another's thinking requires the knotting of one's own thoughts. *I know you have a crush on me. You want to watch me. You want to look at me.*

This sounds familiar. When children are teased, especially when it's boys teasing girls, adults will often use crushes to explain away the trouble. *He is pestering you* (or worse) *because he likes you.* But Wes was the bully, not the bullied. Right? His taunting, sing-song tone about an invented crush drags me back to the '90s, to the too-bright, too-loud hallways of my high school, expressions like *that's so gay* and *no homo* thrown around recklessly and with the intention of harm.

Jim stood behind Wes as he confronted my husband. The camera above them, red light blinking as it steadily recorded the action. I continued to watch from our living room, my gaze realizing them not as objects of desire, but more like characters in a television drama. Onscreen they became small, less villainous, less real.

Out in the driveway, Wes's presumption that my husband is a cisgendered straight man led to a belief that he could wield power over him by jeopardizing that identity with a homophobic taunt. *I know you have a crush on me* is a threat of exposure, recontextualizing the camera not as a security device but a sexual one. Although that part of Wes's mocking rant was incorrect, he was right about the second part. *You want to watch me. You want to look at me.* He did want to. We both did. I wanted to catch them in the act of trespass so that someone might hold them responsible and make them stop.

I watched my husband and the two brothers who tormented us on our television screen, which is not actually a screen but a mixture of glass, color filters, and a liquid crystal polymer. I could have, and had up until the camera went up, been watching them through the window. Even when Wes accosted me in the car there was glass between us. I hadn't stopped to think before about the fragility of what separated me from them.

◉ ◉ ◉

The summer before ninth grade I had to put together a bug collection for my honors earth science course. For months I scooped green beetles out of my neighbor's pool filter, burned the tips of my fingers retrieving singed moths from candle wax, gently removed ladybug husks from the spiderwebs in our basement. I was supposed to affix their bodies to a board that would be placed inside a display case, organized and labeled by order, genus, and species. But those already dead bugs were too stiff with rigor mortis to splay without breaking. The only way to do this project correctly was to catch them alive, kill them swiftly, and pin them before they folded in on themselves. My chest filled with ache. A monarch caught under a glass, a cotton ball drenched in rubbing alcohol.

On the first day of school, we leaned our displays in front of the classroom windows—dead bugs looking out at those still living. The teacher, a six-foot, three-inch tall White man with a bushy mustache and rectangular glasses walked up and down in front of them, staring, rubbing his arms, making humming sounds. He lived next door to the library and was a runner, always in terribly short shorts. When we moved from bugs to geology, he made endless uncomfortable jokes about rocks. *Hot schist. Gneiss cleavage.* I laughed every time, not because I thought his jokes were funny, but because I couldn't let him know he'd made me feel uncomfortable. Laughing was cooler than looking away.

We moved from entomology to geology to zoology. At the end of the year, we presented short reports on the life cycle of an animal of our choosing. I chose the elephant and waited until the last minute to take notes from the *World Book Encyclopedia* onto index cards. *After the rains, bull elephants produce copious amounts of the hormone musth, which increases their sex drives and makes them aggressive.* Fourteen years old, desperate to please, and without a clear understanding of the differences between sex and love, I made a bad pun about the hormone causing the bulls to feel that they "musth" fight or fall in love. My elephant joke was not the same as his rock joke. As I stood behind his broad desk, the teacher scolded me, said there was no way to know what an elephant felt, that transposing human feelings onto animals was both incorrect and unprofessional. *Anthropomorphism is not only wrong, but dangerous for science.* My face reddening, I wished I could leave the room, the school, the whole town. Up, up, away.

Fly: v. To travel through the air. This word is as old as Beowulf, both as a verb and as a name for a winged insect.

Dreaming about flying is common, and analysts link these dreams to thoughts of freedom. Everyone wants to fly, though no one wants to be a fly.

"I have trouble repressing a reflex of shame," writes Jacques Derrida in *The Animal That Therefore I Am*, on his way to thinking about nudity, his cat, and the shame he believes separates human and nonhuman animals. He is not alone in his trouble. Shame is embarrassment's more intense sibling. Embarrassment affects the part of us concerned with our self-image, our outward selves. Shame is more personal, lasts longer, and feels more intense. In front of the class, I was first embarrassed, concerned about how I looked to my classmates. Even now, recalling that day, I feel my insides folding over, ashamed not just at the joke or the chastisement, but by my desire to be liked, a desire that comes from being a teenager, sure, but also from being a woman. I wanted, felt I needed, that man's approval.

After my elephant presentation, I slouched down at my desk near the door, replaying the teacher's assertions in my head on a loop. Twenty-nine years after ninth grade, I am still unwilling to draw a hard line between my emotions and those of nonhuman

animals. Who is he to say there is no romantic love, or some manifestation as such, in nonhuman animals? (Though, who am I to
argue that there is?) Darwin argued there is continuity between
the emotional lives of humans and those of other animals, that
differences between animals and human animals vary in degree
rather than kind. Once, a keeper in the Zoological Gardens told
him about an old Indian elephant shedding tears after her young
one was taken away.[3]

Peacock: v. To puff up with vanity, to make vain, to strut
about and pose, to make oneself a display. Only the male
peacock has that famous tail. Humans associate the bird's
beauty with vanity, but he was born with it.

In Australia, *to peacock* means to obtain the best
portions of a tract of land, especially to make the remainder
of the surrounding land of lower value to other people.
There are so many different types of vanity.

But before Darwin, seventeenth- and eighteenth-century
European naturalists were confused by the existence of apes. They
noticed human similarities, but instead of examining what made

apes apes they "...saw little more than themselves and their own habits mirrored in nature." And so, female apes were understood to be creatures of modesty, males to be violent and capable of rape.[4] These attributes aren't true, of course; these naturalists saw what they wanted to see.

And this must be how Wes arrived at his assumption that my husband's sense of self could be damaged by questioning his cisgendered, straight masculinity. Perhaps he saw in my husband something familiar, maybe Wes's taunt was an attempt to regain imagined power with a show of masculine superiority that would send Matt inside our house, ashamed and defeated, to take down the camera Wes felt threatened by. (To be clear, I am not assuming Wes's straightness, just noticing that regardless of Wes's sexuality, he was using these power dynamics to assert dominance.)

Derrida claims shame isn't in the state of being nude, but in being seen nude. "Nothing will have ever given me more food for thinking through...than these moments when I see myself seen naked under the gaze of a cat,"[5] he writes. At first, this seems to contradict the line I drew before between shame and embarrassment, since he is talking of the hot feeling that rises inside a body after being perceived in a way that feels incorrect or unfair. But the cat, I think, means more to Derrida than even my fellow freshmen meant to me in that science class. You can tell because he keeps coming back to her. We look at animals all the time, especially those who live with us. And they also look at us. Right now, my dog is lying on the couch next to me. Every time I move, he opens his big yellow eyes. He seems to me to be annoyed and I feel badly for irritating him awake, so I tell him I am sorry, explain that I am trying to work, but he huffs and moves further away. It is not enough to simply be seen. We want to be seen and understood. For Derrida, seeing himself being seen by the cat is an act of tables turning. The philosopher becomes the subject of another's thinking, and he cannot access the interpretation.[6]

I, too, feel stuck on the idea of seeing oneself seen.

Gander: v. Older than the verb *to swan*, though the meaning
is the same: to wander aimlessly, in body or in speech. But
also to look at, as in "take a gander." Looking can be violent,
as in staring. The "taking" of a look also implies a lack of
consent. A gander is a male goose. (See also *goose*.)

Remember the story of Wes and Jim's father? How he was
exiled from his home by his wife and sons? Doors locked, all his
belongings in the front yard. When Jean-Paul Sartre writes of
shame, he says "What I apprehend immediately when I hear the
branches crackling behind me is not that there is someone there;
it is that I am vulnerable, that I have a body which can be hurt,
that I occupy a place and that I can not in any case escape from the
space in which I am without defense—in short, that I am seen."
Seen, and also vulnerable. Derrida, too, vulnerable in his nudity
as well as in the gap between understood and understanding. It is
hard to be soft.

I wonder if the brothers and their mother watched through
the windows. If they saw their father pick his underwear off the

hedge and stuff it into his pocket. Or maybe his wife left the curtains closed, let him stand there alone looking down. A small dignity, then, in being unseen, at least by those who were supposed to love him. I wonder whether he drove away with squealing tires or backed slowly down the driveway before driving around the block to see if they changed their minds. And, who knows? Maybe he caught a glimpse of his sons in his rearview mirror, saw himself seen, and smiled with relief rather than shame.

I wonder, too, if Wes knew I was watching him on TV as he yelled at Matt that day in the driveway. If he imagined himself seen by me, his spit flying from the gaping hole in his face, newspapers threatening to spill from the drug store plastic bag in his hand. Is that why he acted the way he did? A performance for an audience of me? Knowing I would understand his actions, knowing that I could read in his flailing and yelling his desire for power, for control, even as he lost it? If I made a sound, would he have realized his vulnerability? Would I have stopped? Our old dog never wagged her tail when she saw them.

◎ ◎ ◎

The European naturalists seeing themselves in apes were worried about what those similarities meant for their understanding of humanness, so they searched for differences that proved human superiority. *Can they think? Can they walk upright? Do they have language? Can they create culture?* They asked these questions because their senses of self had been made wobbly by an expanding awareness of the world.

Their answers often brought them back to ancient ideas about reason: Aristotle's declaration that humans shared a third of their souls with animals;[7] Augustine of Hippo's affirmation that reason is a gift from God setting humans and animal apart; the hierarchy of beings that placed humans between angels and beasts.[8] This thinking concluded that animals lack the ability to reason, that what separates us from them is the ability to understand the purpose of our actions. To justify.

And it's not just that the White European naturalists assumed only human animals can reason, or that this reason makes them superior, but they used this line of thinking to subjugate, enslave, display, and dehumanize people who were not White Europeans by aligning nonwhite, nonmale, non-Europeans with animals, therefore pushing themselves to the top of the hierarchy they invented.

Leanne Betasamosake Simpson writes that human existence is "...ultimately dependent upon intimate relationships of reciprocity, humility, honesty, and respect with all elements of creation, including plants and animals."[9] The naturalists could have looked for interconnectedness or examined behaviors that might have helped them learn differences rather than inferiority. And though this may all seem like ancient history, the posthumanists today who look at how we are enmeshed with the world all too frequently ignore how their thinking is deeply ingrained in generations of Indigenous knowledge. Even in attempts to change colonizer thinking, their hierarchy remains.

I spent this morning watching short videos of animals befriending other animals. A coyote and a badger travel together through a concrete tunnel. A yellow lab and a cheetah cohabitate in a zoo, a deer protects a kitten in a field. My high school science teacher would reason that these interactions were not friendships, but merely matters of circumstance or survival. But I would rather think about what is possible. What is friendship but a coexistence of circumstance, a collaboration in survival?

◎ ◎ ◎

Wes and Jim had a long history of dominating this neighborhood—name-calling, shoving, dumping trash, walking through yards—and before we moved in, they thought they had the money, and therefore the power, to buy this house and take up more space.

But it didn't work. We moved in and prevented their plan for future expansion.

As they stood in the driveway, taunting my husband, it was not only clear they did not want us there, but the camera challenged the hierarchy they had established. I watched as it dawned on them they were going to be watched much in the same way they had previously watched us. They could not see themselves as I saw them, nor did I want to see myself through their eyes. But I realized, in all of this looking, none of us could see ourselves.

When my ninth-grade science teacher told me elephants can't feel love, he was reaching backward through history to maintain an idea about human animal supremacy. Anthropomorphism has a long history of being frowned upon in science circles, a form of "scientific blasphemy" where studies of animal feelings are considered "embarrassing" and "more of a woman's thing."[10] Maybe my teacher skipped the Darwinian writings about elephants' grief. Or passed over them to avoid his own school-related embarrassment.

After going to the dentist to have a cavity filled, my son, who is no longer small, called out for me from the back room of our house, which was once a sun porch but is now where his computer is. It has three walls of windows, and one of them is cracked, the result of a poorly positioned ladder. Even though he is taller than me, even though his voice is deep, I can tell when he needs me. I read that fetal cells can stay inside a mother's body for decades, and perhaps this is why I cannot play it cool when he hurts—why my heart beats faster and my steps become quick and urgent. I am more empathetic to his suffering than anyone else's. He called out to me and I went into the backroom with a bottle of pain reliever. Every twenty minutes I returned to him, interrupting video games and text messages to look at that swollen face, feel for fever, again and again until the swelling went down and his pain ceased. That night I slept fitfully, dreaming of teeth and then waking, straining to listen for any noises across the hall.

Derrida's examination into the differences between human animals and nonhuman animals pushed beyond shame, looked backward to those ancient ideas about reason, and landed on the question *Can they suffer?* The suffering of animals was long dismissed by science, which is how experiments on them went nearly unchecked for years. But I want you to know that elephants have also been known to slow their walking to accommodate herd members in need. They also grieve—a mother elephant will carry her dead calf, and orphaned babies who witnessed their family's poaching screamed at night. Not only do they suffer, but they recognize the suffering of others.

Lately, Matt and I have been watching *Secrets of the Elephants* on National Geographic. Thai elephants stop sugar cane trucks mid-route and use their trunks to lift what they want from the truck beds into their mouths. As I watched them eat their fill, the voiceover tells me that they know not to get greedy, that if they don't take too much, the drivers will let them be, happy to have kept them out of the fields. They are not afraid of anthropomorphizing. Earlier this summer, a story circulated about an elephant in India who killed a woman and then returned to her funeral to trample her corpse, her home, and her livestock. No one can say for certain why this happened. Some have guessed the woman was part of a group of poachers. Others have theorized the woman is Adivasi, an Indigenous group being forced to live too close to elephant habitats.

Vengeance, another type of love, often springs from a desire to protect someone from suffering.

◎ ◎ ◎

The homophobia Wes hurled at my husband was not a vengeance grown from a desire to protect, but rather an attempt to gain power, an act that has historically worked. June told us once that Wes and Jim had a confrontation with Mr. Gallagher, a man who lived in our house decades before. During that confrontation,

Wes backed him up against a car, but Mr. Gallagher pushed him. Wes had him arrested for assault. In our driveway, with the camera recording, Wes got close to my husband. But Matt, who knew the story of Mr. Gallagher's arrest (and also went to a high school where homophobia was bandied about), just turned and walked away. Back inside our house, we watched them on the television together, though closed the windows to shut out their voices. Inside our living room, looking out, we felt somewhat triumphant even though we knew we wouldn't be able leave the house until they drove away. From then on, whenever we saw them trespassing, we hit record, their shadowy bodies stored on a thumb drive. Evidence compressed into data. But if we were beholden to the TV, which one of us was more like the bugs trapped beneath the glass? I keep thinking there must be a straight answer, a clear line through to understanding, but—

Squirrel: v. To go around in circles. To save or hoard.

A list of things I have squirreled away includes: seashells, notes from my husband, bad dreams, old photographs, my son's baby teeth, vintage postcards.

Squirrel fur was coveted in medieval Europe, and was, perhaps, how leprosy was transferred from animal to human. A postmortem revenge.

Sometimes the retelling of Wes and Jim makes me ashamed, and that shame comes in part from worrying I did something wrong. More often lately, talking about them makes me angry—at the ways they invaded our physical space and my thought-space, at my inability to do something, anything, to get them to leave. I feel a throbbing behind my eyes, sometimes I bite my nails. "No one can deny the suffering, fear, or panic, the terror or fright that can seize certain animals and that we humans can witness,"[11] writes Derrida. If I refuse the hierarchy of human animals over animals, if instead I can see myself in relation to them, I understand the body reacts in response to *and* as a reaction. When Matt stood next to me to watch them on TV, his face flushed. I reached over and held his hand.

While we watched them on the screen, Wes and Jim continued gesturing at the camera. I waited for them to spit or throw mud at our house, but they didn't. Eventually they tired themselves out and left. We watched this, too, noticing that Wes's hat was suddenly missing, Jim's shirt had come untucked. Darwin also wrote of animal anger, cataloging how their hair stands on end, their feathers fluff. When upset, apes and monkeys, like humans, turn red, snarl their lips to show their canines. In humans, he writes, anger can even lead to heart attack. But nowhere does he say that nonhuman animals' anger leads them to their own death. They know how to reel it in.

VI. On fear

to hawk

MY FAMILY MOVED A LOT WHEN I WAS GROWING UP. FOR the most part, we stayed in the same town. We even lived on the same street three different times. That street was lined with two kinds of houses: high-roofed Cape Cods and single-story ranches, nearly all built between 1948 and 1952. Behind these houses, scraggly pine trees grew in strips of woods, all the way down the hill where a left turn curved into a dead end. On a map, that neighborhood resembles a hook.

Each time we lived on this street it was in a Cape. My neighborhood best friend Jenny lived in a ranch. When we were closest, we were ten, eleven, twelve, thirteen. She had a pool, her own room, only one younger sibling. Her mother bought brand name snacks and they had a fridge in their basement filled with sodas in glass bottles. I had no pool, two sisters and a brother, and shared my room. My mother only bought store brand snacks and didn't allow soda. From 1989 to 1992, I spent much of my time at Jenny's house.

Her parents never said no to sleepovers. Six or eight girls descended upon their carpeted living room, wearing Garfield nightshirts and zipping into hand-me-down sleeping bags. When it got late enough and her little brother and parents were asleep, we watched movies. The gorier and scarier the better. Every girl hushed and huddled, the volume on the wood-framed television turned to barely hearable as Freddy Krueger's/Michael Myers's/ Hannibal Lecter's face filled the screen. We didn't want to wake her family or get ourselves in trouble, so no matter how scared we felt, we didn't scream.

Afterward, our hearts pounding, we dared each other to run outside. Depending on the girls and the weather, sometimes the dare was to run outside naked. There were two options: run completely around the house or run to the edge of the woods and stand still. There was one rule: no flashlights. Young me, running naked beneath the smooth light of our suburban moon, was thrilled by fear. At that time none of us had yet experienced much of anything. At that time, we were still lucky.[1]

My mother didn't know we watched these movies; she wouldn't have allowed me to go. Watching them at Jenny's was a secret. It wasn't just movies, my mother's list of forbiddens included unsupervised mall and movie trips, using public restrooms alone, bedroom telephones, and spending time in houses where parents were not present. When I graduated high school, she bought me two gifts: a very heavy cell phone to be used only in case of emergencies or between the hours of 9 p.m. and 9 a.m., and a self-defense course held in the basement of our town library. She wanted me to be prepared for the violence of men.

◎ ◎ ◎

In *King Kong Theory*, Virginie Despentes writes about her gang rape as an inevitable event. What she means is that up until it happened, it was something that *could* happen. The potential of it beat inside her like an organ. Once it did happen, it stayed part of her but became not something to be ready for, but something to move forward from. I think about this all the time.

Despentes knew, as so many of us know, that not even a woman's body belongs to her. My mother's mothering was a perpetual lesson in preparing for just-in-case, which I see now as another way of understanding who held sway over our bodies. We never walked alone, never left the street without an adult, never told callers if our parents weren't home. We lived in the hook-shaped neighborhood for years, and my mother believed those two dead-ends to be safe. She gifted me those self-defense classes because I would no longer be living at home where she could watch over me.

In her book on female fear, Pumla Dineo Gqola writes of the patriarchal scripts non-men internalize to avoid harm. "Learn to fight so that you know both how to defend yourself effectively and how to inflict the most harm on a man's body. This will keep you safe."[2] My mother and I went to the classes together. A large White man with a closely-clipped goatee wore a full body suit made of gym mats and taught a class of women how to kick him in the groin, how to use our keys and our fingernails as weapons. White men are, historically and consistently, the most likely to commit an act of violence, which means we were taught to fight by a person most likely to hurt us.[3] Self-defense classes are not going to save us, because men's violence is not about us, the non-men trying to stay safe, but about the desire the men putting us in danger have for power and control. As Virginie Despentes says, "But when the day comes that men are afraid of having their dicks hacked off with a box cutter if they force themselves on a woman, they'll learn pretty quickly to control their 'manly' urges, and understand the meaning of the word no."[4]

Despentes was raped when she was picked up hitchhiking. The men who raped her also raped the friend she was traveling with. Traveling with a friend is not an assault preventative. Despentes had a switchblade with her, but she did not use it. At first, because she worried the men would use it against her if they found it. Then, upon reflection, she notes in that moment of violation she felt "Saving [her] own skin didn't give [her] the right to wound a man."[5] Even in the act of violence, we are thinking about politeness, we are concerned about offending the man with the power. We are restrained. No knives, boxcutters, or long fingernails can cut the misogyny out of us. I wonder now whether that class did any good. Whether its impact on my history reinforced the fear my mother had taught me to have. I can tell you about all the times men hurt me and never did it happen in a dark alley. Never did I grab a man by the ears and knee him in the groin while screaming FIRE, never did I press my bitten fingernails into his eyes.

⊙ ⊙ ⊙

I'm thinking now about how Wes and Jim's threats and derisions were attacks on my manners, my mothering. With a sigh of disappointment, Jim said he'd thought I was *a good girl*. Wes, his hands pressed against my car window, kept repeating that my rudeness meant I was a *bad mother*. And though they confronted my husband less frequently—mainly because he was home less often—they questioned Matt's sexuality the day they found the security camera. Their violences were gender-based violences, and gender-based violence creates fear, which is one of the ways male dominance is established and maintained in our patriarchal society. As I spin outward to grasp at all the ways my experiences are part and parcel to a whole history of white patriarchal settler violence, it is not enough to wear a feminist lens. Racism, classicism, and sexism are mutually reinforcing tools of oppression. bell hooks knew there could be no feminism where there is white supremacy, and as Greta Gaard and other ecofeminists have pointed out, the liberation of women is also tied to the liberation of nature—all forms of oppression are now so inextricably linked that liberation efforts must be aimed at dismantling the system itself.

The power of these perpetuated systems of oppression relies on fear, but that fear must also be witnessed. Here is Gqola again, specifically on female fear: "It is a theatrical and public performance of patriarchal policing of and violence towards women and others cast as female, who are, therefore, considered safe to violate. It requires an audience..."[6] The witnessing is done by the oppressors, of course, like my neighbors, or even the monstrously padded man begging our self-defense class to try and knock him down. But the witnessing also happens when those without power watch each other—like those women who hesitated before punching the padded man, and me and my preteen friends holding hands in the dark while watching Michael Myers raise his knife in *Halloween*.

The men who brutalized the women in those movies were a manifestation of what we already felt inside of our bodies, even if we couldn't yet name it. When the movies were over, adrenaline rising in our thin veins, when we dared each other to run outside, leaving our pajamas outside the backdoor, our nakedness felt freeing. We fled the fear we'd shared, not thinking about who might be looking through their windows.

Much has been written about gender and these types of movies, about the masculinity of violence and the misogyny that leads to the final girl, but I am interested in *Halloween* as it pertains to watching. The film opens by making its viewers accessories to murder. You see through the eyes of the six-year-old Michael Myers as he watches his sister and her boyfriend make out on the couch. You watch with him as they go upstairs, as the boyfriend comes back down, hair disheveled. You follow Myers as he gets the knife, heads into his sister's room, where she sits nearly naked and brushing the dishevel from her own hair. It is through young Myers's point of view that you not only witness the stabbing but see it as if you are the one holding the knife.[7] Of course, you are not holding the knife, you are sitting on the other side of the screen, a member of the audience. Fear needs a witness and a perpetrator, and in this scene, you become both.

Halloween is also a slasher movie set within the domestic and suburban space, another touchpoint of familiarity and comfort, which is also what sets us up to be scared. The tension comes from not knowing when the inevitable loss of comfort will come. When I watched with my friends, we were looking at spaces that looked like more affluent versions of our own neighborhoods. Spaces we were taught to aspire to even as we watched them in peril. *It's just a movie*, we told ourselves, though perhaps this is how we began to understand that nowhere is safe from men or violence, even if no one had told us specifically why. *Halloween* scared us because a masked and murderous man breaking into homes and murdering (mostly) young women was, for us, unexpected. Now, I watch the film and find so much more to recognize.

The slasher films we watched fictionalize the reality of the white flight that led to the rise in the suburb and the parents, like mine, who misplaced their fear onto cities. *Halloween*, like so many movies like it, points out that the danger is on their dead-end streets. The truth was, and is, that danger does not exist only in the dark alleys of big cities, but that men harm women everywhere, that the façade of suburban safety is exactly that.

I rewatched this movie yesterday with Matt, needing to remind myself why it has become synonymous with Wes and Jim in my mind. I thought at first it was all the watching, that I somehow remembered this film begins with looking, and that was what felt familiar. And then I remembered. The last time I watched *Halloween* was the summer I took a horror film and theory class. My mother watched our son while Matt worked in Manhattan and I went to class in the Bronx.

Wes and Jim had quickly learned our schedules, timed their visits to match our comings and goings. And because she was our babysitter, this meant they also knew my mother's.

Once, while not in the horror film class but rather a Social Darwinism in American Literature course, my mother called.

In class, we were discussing *McTeague*, and it was just before our break. She left me a message. *They're here*, she said, *and they are yelling from their side of the driveway.* My mother knew a little of the troubles we had with the brothers, though not all. She knew that they followed Matt to the train, that they were in our backyard, in our driveway, in our heads. I called her back. *We're inside and we're fine*, she said, *but they are standing at the edge of the front yard. They keep pacing in front of your house and stopping at your walkway.* Like with my son, whenever I talked to her about Jim and Wes, I masked my concern. Whether I did that to keep her from worrying about our safety, or because I was ashamed that we had chosen the wrong house, or because we couldn't afford to lose her as our caregiver, I can't be sure. It was probably a mix of the three. I never mentioned the brothers to my grad school cohort. I told my mother to call the police. She did, but by the time they showed up, Wes and Jim had left. Twice a week for two years they pulled up at the same time she did, meeting her in the driveway after she picked up my child from the daycare next door. They called her by her first name, even though she'd never been introduced.[8]

In the years we lived beside them, neither brother ever physically harmed us. The closest they came was trapping us in the car. They never threatened physical harm, either. But their bodies became a constant and foreboding presence at the periphery. Always too close, yet far enough away they evaded any punishment. Wes frequently reminded us the first three feet at the front of a property belong to the city, regardless of whether or not there is a sidewalk, so when they paced by our front porch, they were not breaking any laws. Pinning me in the car was terrifying, but I had no way to prove any harm was done. So much can be dismissed as coincidence. So much can be reframed as misperception. So much gets brushed away, unprovable.

It wasn't just their physical presence. Their words, too, were threatening. Sometimes, these threats were litigious. *If you film us, we will sue you.* Other times they were lies. *We see you walking in our yard, too.* Often they were coded as benign, but invoked fear by revealing they were watching, researching. *Hello, Amie ELIZABETH*, they'd say, emphasizing and stretching out my middle name. Once, Wes said he had met my ex-husband and that he was *a pretty nice guy*. Of course, I had never told him I was divorced.

◎ ◎ ◎

In *Halloween*, Laurie first sees Michael Myers in a car in a parking lot. It is the act of staring that scares her in the beginning. Laurie then sees Myers in the bushes, but when her friend peers behind the shrub line he is gone. She's always the only one. I recognize her fear. It is the fear of violence in potentia.

Sometimes I try to convince myself it wasn't that bad. They just followed me. Only trapped me in my car once. Only shouted. Only stared. If *Halloween* was a film about Laurie knowing she was being followed and watched and no one was murdered, it would still be scary, but she would be perceived as "crazy," as "hysterical." Instead of a slasher about teens knifed post-sex by an escaped mental patient, it would be a movie about the abundance and predictability of female madness. She is a woman scared of a man she should be afraid of, but no one, at first, will believe her. Until it's too late. Do you see what I am trying to say?

◎ ◎ ◎

"How we live together influences how we look at one another and what we expect to see,"[9] writes Rosemarie Garland-Thomson about staring, and I think about all the ways I have looked and been looked at. The look of love, which is different from the look of lust. The be-quiet look from a parent to a child, and the stop-looking-at-me look between siblings. Wes and Jim's staring, though, was a different kind of look. Their looks, provocative and paralyzing, if we remember Garland-Thomson, were what sent me nailing towels to the windows when we first moved in. What Wes and Jim were doing when they stood in our house/in our backyard/on our side of the driveway was asserting their power as well as our powerlessness.

But it isn't fair to only say that Wes and Jim were villains and I their female victim. They wanted our house, sought to stake their claim over more of this neighborhood. To get what they wanted, they tried to intimidate us into leaving by following, lurking, and staring at us. And their staring was not just a rude deviation from social codes. Wes and Jim's staring was representative of a masculine desire for dominance, a veiled aggression meant to put me/my husband/my mother in our place. But they weren't the only leering bad guys. I stared at them, too.

Here's the difference. I stared at them from inside our house, from within the confines of our property. I peeked from behind curtains and watched from the attic, checking incessantly to see if they had pulled into the driveway. I also watched them mow and weed their lawn, even when they were nowhere near my own. I stared at their house, snuck looks into their car windows whenever I had the chance. My staring, though still a violation of social code, still an affront to generations of advice to *mind my own business*, was intended as a means of protection and meant to be kept private.

My protective, private staring came from fear and a manifestation of my own internalized misogyny. It felt impossible to stare at Jim and Wes openly the way they stared at me, a modified eye-for-an-eye, not because I could not meet their dominance or aggression, but because I feared it would send the wrong message, a message of welcome, or attraction, or interest. My looking might not be perceived as power, but as flirtatiousness. The brothers' dominating glare "act[ed] out the gendered asymmetries of patriarchy,"[10] and so, as I perched in my attic, my failure to meet their gaze allowed them to hold onto a hierarchy where they already sat at the top. Even if I had met their gaze, though, the hierarchy wouldn't have changed.

This dominance staring is part of what Laura Mulvey explains in her theory of the male gaze, which also explains why the murdered babysitters in *Halloween* are nearly nude, in bed or recently out of it, and conventionally attractive. But staring isn't only about dominance and sex, or being the dominant sex. Staring is steeped in understandings of class that can be traced back to George Washington and through nineteenth century pamphlets on manners.[11] Along with rise of industry and the birth of the middle class, in the nineteenth century Americans also shifted their understandings of privacy. Strangers now lived close together. Families that used to exist as self-contained systems had to learn boundaries to coexist. Gentlemen (who were, of course, part of the public) were taught not to stare at women (because the domestic space is private). Therefore, starers were disobeyers of society's expectations. Only the lower class stared.

The shift in industry and class consciousness led to a rethinking not only of how to live and how to look in the city, but also whether the city was the ideal place to call home at all. Though the suburb is often equated with post–WWII Levittowns, suburban living came from England more than fifty years earlier, when William Wilberforce, an evangelical preacher and crusader for the abolition of slavery believed that the rising industrialization of London was cause for alarm. In short, he believed the city to be "bad," physically and morally, and proclaimed women and children should be moved into a more "wholesome" environment. The idea of "badness" came from a fear of women in public, more specifically, that a woman who was not a prostitute would be mistaken for one.[12] This fear, not just of being mistaken for a woman getting paid for sex, but of women being sexual at all is still baked into our culture. When I turned eleven and wanted to shave my legs, my mother told me to stop at my knees because "only easy girls shave higher than that." A few years later, while getting ready to go out with my high school friends, she warned me not to go out "dressed like that." In slasher movies, the survivor is always the woman who hasn't had sex.

Wilberforce's ideas came to America just as fear-driven. To sell them, they presented the suburb as a hub for women's safety, a respite from the crowding and filth they should be protected from.[13] Advertisements used gender-coded descriptions masked as hope, describing suburbia's cleanliness and ample space by using words like *wholesome* and *domestic*. Here is "chronicler of city growth," Adna F. Weber's 1899 description: "The 'rise of the suburbs' . . . furnishes the solid basis of a hope that the evils of city life, so far as they result from overcrowding, may in large part be removed."

Hawk: v. To pursue or attack while flying.
To sell in the street by yelling about one's wares.

The Cape Cods and ranches that made up the neighborhood I grew up in are an example of the post–WWII Levittowns targeted toward veterans. These three-bedroom, one-bathroom homes came furnished with appliances, each built upon a standardized, manicured plot of land, all lined up like the soldiers they were built for. Beyond these streets were the schools, grocery stores, and businesses necessary for a town, though they were all built with miles of road between them, requiring these households to have at least one car, creating an environmental nightmare atop the white patriarchal ideals of a new wave of settler colonization.[14]

The homogeneity of the Levittown suburb extended to its residents. Though touted as accessible housing for veterans, these neighborhoods intentionally left Black families out, regardless of military service. Not only did they refuse to sell to Black families, but, like the White colonizer settlers of centuries prior, the construction of the suburb relied often on Black people's labor. This is not to say that Black people have not or are not living in suburbs. In 2015, the New York Public Library hosted the *Black Suburbia* exhibit.[15] This is where Doria Johnson, a doctoral candidate in history at the University of Wisconsin and the assistant curator of the exhibition's sections on Compton and Baldwin Hills, wrote about how lynchings drove many Black families, including her own, from the South to the suburbs up north. At the time of the most recent census, most African Americans live in the suburbs. It is White people who see the suburb as a white place. And white supremacy has perpetuated the idea that people of color are outsiders in these neighborhoods. As I write this chapter, a Black sixteen-year-old boy named Ralph Yarl is recovering from gunshot wounds in Missouri. Andrew Lester, the White man who shot him did so because the boy rang the wrong doorbell. He was trying to pick up his younger brothers.

Suburbia promised idyll to White people. It promised a heteronormative nuclear family that shifted the veteran into a nine-to-five businessman and his wife to a stay-at-home mom with her hands full of house upkeep. These neighborhoods still exist, and for many signify success.[16] However, as Leslie Kern explains in *Feminist City*, since they were built to last, we are stuck with neighborhoods that still reflect these troublesome ideals. Of course, this way of life isn't even indicative of most families, especially families of color, the working class, and LGBTQIA+ families. The sustained existence of suburban spaces perpetuates these gender roles and, as Kim TallBear tells us in her talk "Disrupting Settlement, Sex, and Nature," further dispossesses the Indigenous Peoples to whom this land belongs, because of the ways these neighborhoods enforce monogamy and the boundaries of private property on Indigenous people.[17] Suburbs have been created through displacement, racism, and misogyny. No wonder so many horror films take place here.

◉ ◉ ◉

To write about Wes and Jim then is to write about my own suburban horror movie. To think about why they acted the way they did is to hold up anecdotal evidence of white patriarchal power. Why was I so afraid when neither brother physically harmed me? Though they followed, infringed, and shouted, neither laid a hand on me. For a moment, I worry that I may have made a big deal about nothing.

This bears repeating: Instilling fear is a way of maintaining power, or extracting more power, or removing someone else's power. Fear is meant to be constant because it is integral to patriarchy and white supremacy, underpinning traditions of oppression and containment.[18] My fear is mine and is also part of a collective consciousness, held by many folks living outside of a cisgendered straight White male identity. I am a cisgendered White woman and so have tremendous privilege, though still feel this fear. Like an electrical undercurrent to our existence, the longer it's felt, the more we grow accustomed to it. Kern explains that since we can't control where the men responsible for our fear are, we displace that fear from men to places: the dark alley, the city street. But we know that most violence occurs at home.[19] With Jim and Wes in our shared driveway or in our yard, the displaced fear became real and the violence more possible.

My fear, like Despentes's, comes from understanding that not even my body is my own. What I mean is, my fear is tied to sexual assault, the never-fading potential for that act to happen, for someone to claim rights to my body. Everyday experiences of male dominance and past experiences with assault mean that there is always a fear of future assaults, a reinforced understanding that I don't belong in certain spaces. Perhaps in *any* spaces. This, coupled with a childhood socialization to fear both men and public spaces, means that every screech of their car, each step into our yard, each steely glare into our windows, and every boom of their voices affirmed the possibility that our neighbors could do something and would likely not be held accountable for whatever it is they'd do. Their words, as Gqola explains, are their actions.

And so, like the girl-me who watched slasher movies in a dark living room, I watched Jim and Wes from the attic, silent, knowing we could not leave this house—because of the impossibility of upheaving our child, the financial burden, and our inability to conceive of foisting this situation upon another family. I dreamed of luring them into the woods, stripping them bare and leaving them. In the mornings I whispered these dreams to my husband, embarrassed by my desire for revenge. He listened, apologized sometimes, though I am not sure for what. I think it was for leaving, for going to work, though maybe it was for his gender, or for the way their behavior took up so much of my headspace. And the truth was, I was sorry, too. Sorry I couldn't do something, sorry I couldn't fight or flee, sorry I couldn't forget. Together, we worried about the little boy down the hall who had, in his little life, watched his parents get divorced, moved house, and switched schools. Could he sense we were still unsettled, or had all the unsettle that had already happened made this feel, somehow, normal?

Downstairs, we had a kitchen full of knives, but I knew I could never bring myself to cut the two men staring at me from the edge of my backyard.

VII. On boundaries, again

to seal/to lark/to wolf

WES AND JIM TOLD US THEY WANTED THIS HOUSE, HAD tried to buy it and had offered Jerry cash, but Jerry refused to sell to them. We thought Jerry's rejection was our good luck, or maybe an act of loyalty given we'd filed the paperwork first, but perhaps he was trying to protect the neighborhood from an expansion of their greed. Or maybe it was spite.

And so, Jerry's rejection first became our good fortune and then became our misfortune. We asked ourselves over and over, how much could we withstand before we had to move?

Walking out of the library one day early in the semester, Maggie, who lives on the other side of us and was not as frequently a target of the neighbors' misdeeds, sent me a video of Wes standing in my front yard, his hands around his eyes in makeshift binoculars. She had just retrieved my child from the bus, as she did on days my mother worked late. In the video, I heard his tiny voice asking if I would be home soon. I wish she hadn't sent it. I am glad that she sent it. I wanted to turn around. I needed to get to class.

I sent her a text asking if they were okay. She said they were going inside and would stay there until my mother came.

◉ ◉ ◉

The thing is, we could not move out of this house, but we could not stay either, not like this, not any longer. We needed a fence.

The morning after Maggie sent the video, Matt called a local fence installation company. A woman asked him what type of fence we were looking for (as tall and solid as possible) and then asked for our address. When she typed this information into her computer, all our demographic information appeared. They had installed a fence here before. Why would anyone have taken it down? The woman on the phone said she would send someone out to calculate an estimate.

I was home alone when the man came to measure, arriving in a white van. Jim and Wes's car was already here. I couldn't see or hear them and assumed they were inside. I waved the fence salesman over to the opposite side of our house, psychically begging him to be quiet. He slammed his door shut.

Once around the side of the house beyond where the brothers could see us, I explained our situation. I tried not to cry and failed. The man was White and wore a soft plaid shirt, his mustache cartoonishly wide. He had a clipboard, which he wrote notes on while resting the edge of it on top of his belt buckle. He was patient with me, let me finish unloading a year's worth of angst. *So we'd like to put it up as soon as possible*, I told him. He looked me in the eye and said he understood. He'd been the one to put up the previous fence, said he was shocked it was no longer up and also not at all surprised we needed it to be replaced. When he walked the property line, Wes and Jim watched from their driveway. I waited in the house, my arms across my chest, hands on my own shoulders. Wes and Jim said nothing, only stared from their side of the driveway. The man from the fence company said he would call soon with the cost.

The estimate they gave us came with a caveat. They would not install our fence unless we called our local precinct and requested police assistance. During the previous installation, Jim and Wes had harassed the men putting in the fence, so much so that they refused to come back without protection. Privacy, we learned, is expensive.

It would be one week before they could put the fence in, and the brothers showed up every day. They complained to other neighbors that we were ruining the sightline of the neighborhood, that we were stealing their property, that we could not be trusted not to move the (already stolen) property marker. When I left the house, Wes gloated through a threat, *You thought you could do this without us knowing, but you didn't. You can't get away with this. You won't.*

Seal: v. To close (with a seal). If an agreement is sealed with a handshake, that agreement is considered binding. You can press a seal to close something up; to seal wood, use varnish. *To seal* is to smother.

In elementary school in the late '80s/early '90s, we swapped valentines stamped with the wet-sounding acronym SWAK, which meant sealed with a kiss.

The night after the fence installation, the brothers walked up and down their side of the new fence with measuring tapes, flashlights, and an iPad. They kicked the fence over and over, not hard enough to do any damage, but hard enough that I could hear them from where I watched in the attic, taking photos. I was sure they would destroy it as we slept, so I watched until late into the night, until they finally got into their cars and drove away.

For weeks after, whenever they saw us, whenever they saw anyone, they would talk about how grateful they were that *they* had the fence put in. How they couldn't believe *they* had waited so long, that *they* were so relieved to have finally found a way to keep *us* off their property. Sometimes I would see them crouched next to it, heads near the ground and looking through the gap between fence and grass.

The fence installation switched from something done to *them* to something they did to *us*, and I am baffled at the swiftness with which the truth disappeared.[1] I expected anger, even destruction. But acceptance seemed doubtful. Ownership impossible.

Our fence did not stop Wes and Jim from walking through other people's yards. They still dropped their lawn clippings and stray twigs onto other people's property. They still walked up and down the street looking at the faces of each house, stopping at ours to linger. We could hear them talking to themselves about how they had gifted the stone gargoyle in the yard or, even stranger, purchased the sink in our bathroom. When Matt was in the backyard with the dog, Wes walked through the backyards of those who live behind us to watch him from where the fence was lower. Although these acts are violating, they (almost) never actually broke the law. Kant, Hannah Arendt says in her lectures on his political philosophy, "thought a bad man can be a good citizen in a good state."

When we put in the fence, we made a hard boundary, a physical barrier between us and them. This gave me a feeling of safety. A fence is a structure of both inclusion and exclusion, a delineation between private spaces and public ones. In a "good" state, a fence might enable privacy. In a bad one, it is an object of Othering, a weapon used to prevent privacy, to refuse asylum. Whether the wall of a fence provides privacy or prevents safety, a humanmade fence is a trap to nonhuman animals who get tangled or cannot pass through the land. A fence can also be a rupture to the natural processes of the earth, stopping migration patterns, winds, or damming up water.

Lark: v. To play tricks, frolic. To ride in a frolicsome manner; to ride across country (as in "lark about").

To ride (a horse) across the country. This makes sense when we also consider that *to lark* has also meant to clear a fence with a flying leap. To lark a fence, one becomes like a horse breaking free from confinement.

Lastly, to make fun of, to tease a person sportively. I think teasing is cruel, as a sport or otherwise.

At the back and alongside our yard farthest away from the brothers' house, the fence we put in is a split rail. A non-fence fence assuring squirrels and chipmunks and possums can still travel freely while also helping us feel less hemmed-in. We can rest our elbows on the top of this fence and talk to our other neighbors. Jim and Wes's yard was now fenced in solidly and completely, since their other neighbors had already installed the same high vinyl fence on their sides. The brothers were surrounded by a view so white and tall it became almost impossible for them to see over either side without standing on a ladder.

Their backyard had become a secret, hidden space. Secrecy is a form of exclusion, a withholding of information, and it has been a tool of male dominance for ages. Heterosexual partner violence is most likely to happen by men in the home, a private space where secrets can be kept in drawers like spoons. How many women spoke out about Harvey Weinstein, or Bill Cosby, or Louis C.K, or Donald Trump before action was taken? How often do those punishments stick? How many more times is action never taken? Private abuses are meant to be kept that way.

One of the things I've learned from those years living beside the brothers is it sometimes isn't enough for men to do harm privately. Sometimes they harm in public, as the brothers did, for an audience (of other men, of police, of neighbors, of strangers) who they know will stand by and watch. This is how men's powers can remain intact, while women's bodies are continuously broken. María Pía Lara, writing on male dominance in public spaces, explains how Habermas's theorizing about the public sphere helps us understand how exclusion enables male domination. "White men had structured a kind of rationality that made their particular perspective appear as if it were the universal form of inclusion and representation."[2] The public sphere was and is a performance space for male ideas. Public opinion often discredits women's stories. The public eye is infected with the male gaze, and this is why women who speak out about violence or harm are called liars or are found at fault for whatever heinous act they survive.

Another horror film, *The Texas Chain Saw Massacre* (1974), among other things is a surreal and apocalyptic film about capitalism and meat. In it, a group of teens is murdered and eaten by a family of butchers-turned-cannibals after the economy takes a turn and they lose their slaughterhouse jobs. Early in, there is a scene where Pam, looking for her boyfriend, disappears inside the old farmhouse where the cannibals live. When no one answers the door, she stumbles inside, disoriented and afraid. The house seems off-kilter as she falls into a room that might be called a living room, except all the furniture is made of bones. From the ceiling hangs a human skull ringed with feathers, a horn clenched in its jaw like a cigar. With Pam on the ground, the camera darts between her and a cage suspended from the ceiling. A live chicken paces inside the cage. In rapid succession, the camera jerks back and forth between Pam's terror-stricken face and the bird above, who similarly twitches her eyes and darts around in her cage. The audience is presented with a strange parallel. Pam and the chicken share similar body language, erasing the separation between human and non-human animal, and we understand that for the cannibals, both are meat. As Pam frantically surveys the room, so does the bird, their eyes correspondingly darting in their heads. Pam is also aware she is trapped. In these moments of visceral terror, Pam does not scream.[3] She dry heaves and tries to run away. As she does, Leatherface grabs her and methodically hangs her on a meat hook before returning to the butchering of her boyfriend's corpse. "Fragmentation of the human body in late capitalism allows the dismembered part to represent the whole,"[4] writes Carol J. Adams in *The Sexual Politics of Meat*. Pam is a victim of violence inside a house where no one can hear her. Inside the cannibals' home, she is no longer a living woman, but another piece of meat, trapped and hung.

The Texas Chain Saw Massacre ends with a dinner scene. The cannibal men sit around the table, like a horrible recreation of Norman Rockwell's *Freedom from Want*. Now the camera focuses on Sally, another teen from the road trip, who is alive but bound and gagged at the table. In front of her lies a taxidermized chicken's head and feet—dismembered parts meant to represent the whole. I assume these parts came from the chicken that earlier hung in the living room above Pam. This means that in this murder house, what cannot be eaten is turned into art, a different kind of consumption.

Wolf: v. To devour ravenously. (See also *pig*.)

In one version of the story of the three little pigs, a wolf destroys the first two pigs' homes and eats them, a punishment for their laziness. But the reason the pigs were on their own to begin with is because their mother didn't have enough food to feed them. Really, then, they are products of a failed system. In some other versions of this story, the lazy pigs aren't eaten but escape to the house where their responsible brother lives, and the three cook up the wolf and eat him for dinner.

Earlier, when writing about an encounter with Wes, I said I felt like a piece of meat. When someone says this, likely not a man, likely after a boundary has been breached, they are using a visceral metaphor to explain the feeling of being made both abject and object. It isn't so much about the meat, but about how the act of violence felt. In *The Texas Chain Saw Massacre*, this metaphor is made real. Within this metaphor, too, is a racial hierarchy. "The truth is—in sexist America, where women are objectified extensions of male ego, black women have been labeled hamburger and white women prime rib,"[5] writes bell hooks in *Ain't I A Woman*.

◉ ◉ ◉

I do not make New Year's resolutions. It's too much pressure, it's too dark and too cold in January to make lifestyle changes. But four months into living here, on our first New Year's in this house, we stopped eating meat. We had been talking about it for months, had already quit fish, seldom had beef. We had read a lot about overfishing and about microplastics in seafood, about factory farm practices and the environmental impact of livestock farming and slaughter. The last meat we ate was ham.

The night of our last meat, friends came over to spend the night. Their child and ours were near the same age and were excited to stay up until midnight. We spent most of the evening in our living room where I had recently steamed off the wallpaper, exposing the horsehair plaster beneath. Perhaps it was the vulnerability of the bare walls exposed, but before the ball fell, we confided in these friends, explained what had been happening with the brothers next door. Their mouths hung open. Tommy spent the night checking through the window, Helen peppered us with questions I didn't have the answers to. At the time, I hadn't thought that our switch to vegetarianism had anything to do with Jim and Wes.

Wes and Jim epitomize masculinity's endless hunger for power. Our vegetarianism, then, was both a real and symbolic gesture, a move of self-preservation (we are all meat) but also an attempt to avoid internalizing anymore violence. Though meat eating in many Indigenous cultures is respectful, intentional, and careful, the meat available in suburban grocery stores mostly comes from farming where meat-making practices are unsustainable, reckless, and filled with harm.

Upton Sinclair's novel *The Jungle* sparked a wave of vegetarianism when it came out in 1905. His descriptions of a slaughterhouse in the opening chapters are so visceral that though he intended his story to expose the dark side of labor and capitalism, it was the revelation of *where* meat comes from that struck a chord with his readers.

"I aimed at the public's heart," he wrote in his autobiography, "and by accident I hit it in the stomach." The steps of animal slaughter are carefully detailed: hogs are carried by one foot through the air and onto the conveyor belt where they are killed and turned to sellable meat. There are holes in the floor for unusable parts to fall into, and blood spreads inches-thick on the floor. In this description, Sinclair, too, realizes how metaphor becomes the necessary language for violence. "One could not stand and watch very long without becoming philosophical, without beginning to deal in symbols and similes, and to hear the hog-squeal of the universe."[6]

That hog-squeal of the universe is one of injustice, violence, and death, not just for the nonhuman animals, but also for the human animals in Sinclair's fictional city of Packingtown, where suffering is a cycle and there is a price to being alive, a price on every body. This is made more obvious when Ona and her baby die in childbirth. Jurgis, her husband, just out of prison after assaulting the man who raped her, does not have money for medical aid. Eventually, he finds a midwife who begrudgingly agrees to help her deliver the baby. The midwife is described as fat, as frying pork and onions while Jurgis stands in her kitchen, all important details in a novel where everyone is starving or nearly starving despite their endless production of food. Even with her help, Ona and the baby die. When the midwife tells this to Jurgis, she has "her jacket off, like one of the workers on the killing-beds," which leaves us to understand that the poverty-stricken Ona and her baby are no longer people, but meat, and maybe that's all they ever were. It's been noted that *The Jungle* is filled with dark spaces—slaughterhouses, prisons, attics—and that these dark spaces resemble wombs.[7] In this argument I see another fragmentation of women's bodies. Pieces representing the whole.

So many stories about meat and women, eating and being eaten. It feels endless, men either consuming or shaming women's bodies. Here's another one:

In Sarah Rose Etter's 2019 novel *The Book of X*, the men work in a meat quarry. They rise early to dig into bloody cave walls and remove hunks of meat big enough to sell. The women of the story, a daughter named Cassie and her mother, like her mother before her, do not work in the quarry. Instead, they wash the white walls of their house with lemons. These women are born with knotted torsos, painful twists of flesh that protrude from their sides, so shocking that "The doctors had the same reaction each birth: They lifted our slick warped bodies into the air and stared, horrified. All three of us wailed, strange new animals, our lineage gnarled, aching, hardened."[8] The knots are a painful, visible reminder of the inherited pain of womanhood.

Etter brings the expression "I felt like dead meat" a step further. Beyond the understanding that a living woman might feel like a dead animal prepared for consumption when in the company of men, Etter's characters are emblematic of women's pain, their living meat twisted, their doctors unhelpful and dismissive. It reminds me of all the ways women's health care is overlooked—migraine, endometriosis, PCOS, cancer, menopause, birth trauma, IUD insertion, stroke, heart disease, Lupus, rheumatoid arthritis, depression—but I also want to think about what this story is saying about the land.

In this world, the earth is mined for meat. Though the animal part of meat consumption is eliminated, there is still violence. The men work with tools, sharp picks dig into the walls of flesh and they tear huge glistening chunks off, bring them back to town and sell them, violence turned into profit. A boy rapes a teenage Cassie in the meat cave, a violent act inside of a violent act. Shortly after the attack, she sneaks back to the cave and stuffs her mouth full of meat, as if eating could make her feel whole again, an act of reclamation.

On our last night of meat, I felt I was moving toward something gentler. I had thought much about consumption, about waste and harmful farming practices. In *Braiding Sweetgrass*,

Robin Wall Kimmerer writes, "Whether we are digging wild leeks or going to the mall, how do we consume in a way that does justice to the lives that we take?"[9] This is a question of care.

I cared about what was happening immediately inside my body, inside my house, and also beyond my immediate reach, concentric circles of care and harm crisscrossing into a scribble. So maybe, maybe, giving up meat was an attempt to reclaim some sense of order. I had moved here full of hope, excited to start over with my new husband, with my son. How quickly that was derailed, my sense of self and safety taken, a potential for more violence each time Jim and Wes pulled in the driveway. "One of our responsibilities as human people is to find ways to enter into reciprocity with the more-than-human world. We can do it through gratitude, through ceremony, through land stewardship, science, art, and in everyday practical reverence,"[10] Kimmerer continues. Vegetarianism seemed a way to step away from feeling like I was backed against my own walls, constantly torn between wanting to eat and the fear of being eaten.

VIII. On boundaries, once more

to fish/to ram/to chicken (out)/to duck

IN THE BUTTER LIGHT OF EARLY SUMMER, I SAW A mother house finch teach her fledgling to peck small seeds from the clover in the grass. I watched them, this mother with her baby who was already her size,[1] glad to witness their animal tenderness, even while human animals destroy the planet. A haze of residual wildfire smoke from Canada stings my eyes, my throat. I am writing about violence, about control, about the neighbors who made me feel violent and out of control and I am grateful for these birds who remind me of what is gentle.

The word "gentle" comes from an Anglo-Norman word used to describe someone "of noble or good birth." The Latin root "gene" means "to give birth, to beget." On its path toward its current meaning, "gentle" was used as an adjective to describe animals of excellent stock, with tame or "easily managed" dispositions, and domesticated plants or trees; cultivated, rather than natural. "Gentle" is linked to "gentile" and "gentleman," also "genteel," which was once understood to mean "pertaining to the fairies." The way we use it today, to describe someone with a mild disposition, someone "good-natured" or kind, feels soft. But before softness, it was an adjective of class and prestige, the breaking of living beings into submission. A taming by those with money and status.

◎ ◎ ◎

On my bookshelf is a resin sculpture of the fish woman in René Magritte's 1934 surrealist painting *Collective Invention*. She has the head and torso of a gray fish, the vulva and legs of a White woman. An inverted mermaid, a destabilization of expectations. I love her, though she frightens me a little.

She lies on her left side. Her body is pale gray, iridescent and shimmery before becoming gently beige. There is no distinct line on her belly where she changes from one being to the other. She does not have a navel above the soft darkness of her pubic hair, no visible scales on her fish half. In both painting and sculpture, her black eye looks wet, her mouth slightly open. In the painting, her gills appear sharper, her edges darker as she rests on yellow sand, the waves small behind her. A fish cannot breathe outside of the water. She is drowning.

Magritte's mother died of suicide. Exhausted, unsupported, and living through depression, she once tried to drown herself in a water tank in the cellar her husband had locked her in "for her own protection." Three months after Magritte's thirteenth birthday, his mother got up early and left the bedroom she shared with her youngest son, who slept in there "perhaps as comfort, perhaps as canary."[2] Eighteen days later, her body was found by a dredger in the river. Magritte never spoke about his mother, not even to his wife. And yet, it has been speculated that the paintings *L'Histoire Centrale* (1928) and *L'Inondation* (1928) are influenced by her death. In the former, a woman stands behind a tuba and a suitcase, her face and head completely covered by white fabric, her left hand around her neck. In the latter, the naked bottom half of (the same?) woman stands on a dock, the water behind her, the tuba beneath her left hand. Above her navel, her torso fades away into the blue sky.

Only Magritte's friend, poet and fellow surrealist Louis Scutenaire, seems to have been able to get him to open up about her death. Scutenaire wrote an evocative retelling of the events surrounding the discovery of her body, describing her face as "concealed by her nightdress." It's inaccurate for him to have written as if Magritte and his brothers were there—they weren't—but still, he writes: "They never knew whether she had covered her eyes in order not to see the death that she had chosen."[3] Perhaps, then, he reconstructed his drowned mother as part fish, her naked, human lower half exposed, her missing navel implying a nonexistent relationship to the maternal. She could not be a mermaid; a mermaid could not bear a child. But if this fish woman is his mother, the air would suffocate her. I wonder if he understood how difficult her life had been.

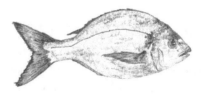

Fish: v. To fish, as a verb, sometimes refers to the act of catching, often with a hook, the noun version. We've named the act of killing fish after the casualty. We fish items out of places—keys from pockets, lost jewelry from sink drains. And we fish for compliments. This usage—fishing as eliciting a response or opinion—can be dated to 1570. In 1986, my uncle swallowed a goldfish whole, right in front of me, and expected me to clap. I called him a monster, wished the fish could swim up and out of his body.

All of this is speculation, an attempt to make connections, to render Magritte's art as a metaphor for his life. For years, I have dug through memories and read through books trying to uncover the reason for Wes and Jim's behavior. What might have happened to them as children to cause them to wield their power this way? Freud blamed mothers for children's pathologies, and if I look to what I know of their mother I wonder whether I will find an actual answer or whether I have simply internalized his theory enough to force what I know into a reason, use his work as a vessel.

Ram: v. To batter. To ram as in to beat down the earth and ram as in a male sheep both appeared in writing around the same time. Now *to ram*, also *to ram in*, evokes a smashing. Ram it in there, ram it with your car. Rams will smash into each other, a fight for dominance.

Also: to force (a bullet, bolt, charge, etc.) into a firearm, usually by means of a ramrod.

We thought installing the backyard fence meant we would no longer be exposed, that Wes and Jim would no longer be able to watch us. My child, almost eight by then, thought that sleeping in a tent would be fun. On a mild evening a few weeks after the fence went up, we arranged for the dog to spend the night with my in-laws, set up the tent, inflated an air mattress, charged the rechargeable batteries for the lanterns, and dragged our sheets and blankets into the backyard.

Against the dusk, the walnut trees' leaves looked like feathers. We set up the tent at the base of the small hill where the hollowed-out crabapple tree once stood,[4] where the ground is flatter, with the door flap facing the back of the yard so that when we unzipped it in the morning, we'd look out at the willow tree instead of at the rear of our house. We left the mesh window open to watch the bats and the fireflies and the sky's progression toward night. By 8:30, it was dark.

At first we brushed off the bright bobbing light as a jogger or maybe someone walking their dog down the street.

It is about sixty feet from the street to the stretch of split-rail fence that encloses the backyard. In the center of it is a gate. There is no way, even in the dark, to accidentally wander to where the gate latches closed. But there was Wes, his elbows bent and resting on the wood, flashlight held up next to his ear, sweeping his beam of light back and forth across the yard.

The loud *What the fuck are you doing Wes?* could have been shouted by either me or my husband. In the dark, we can be brazen. *Wes. You're trespassing.* At first he stayed silent. Perhaps he thought if he remained still we would forget he was there. Behind the brightness of his flashlight, we could not make out his face, we could only squint, our arms over our eyes like characters in a sci-fi movie approaching an alien ship. We held up our phones, yelled *We are taking pictures of you, Wes. We'll call the police, Wes.* And when he still didn't walk away, Matt grabbed a lantern and left the tent.

◎ ◎ ◎

I once had a dream I lost my child. Not lost as in death, but as in misplaced. In the dream I felt panicked, looking from room to room in our house that suddenly had more rooms than it ever had before. When I opened the front door I found him on the porch, small and crying, and I remembered we had been at a bus station and that I'd somehow come home alone. *Did someone hurt you*, I asked, and despite my real-life child being too big to hold, I felt his small nodding head against my shoulder. I gasped myself awake.

As Matt walked toward the fence, soft lantern light wobbling, Wes began to speak. *I'm not doing anything wrong. I'm not. I have every right to know what you are doing back there. It's my right.* But just as Matt got close, Wes turned off his flashlight and walked away.

Watching from the tent, I tried to cover up my worry by making shadow puppets with my hands. The hardest part of mothering is knowing you are too soft to stave off the sharpness of the world. My child, in a tent, in the dark. A man watching us with a flashlight. The fence transformed from an object of protection to one of display. A fence is a frame. We carried on with our plans and stayed in the tent, though neither of the adults were able to fall asleep.

Chicken (out): v. To withdraw from an activity.

Maybe Magritte's *Collective Invention* is less a specific rendering of his mother's death and is instead a broader depiction of sex and death, a painted petite mort. I look at her again, lying there exposed, and am reminded of the high school boys who described vaginas as "smelling like fish." "Dead fish" is an expression used to describe a female partner who lies flat and unresponsive during sex. A dead fish is also meat, though some don't consider it as such, Catholics even allowing it to be eaten during Lent. How many ways can a woman be consumed? How many ways can a fish be a metaphor?

The fish woman of *Collective Invention* is two lives, two beings, attached at their midpoints. She exists both as a fish and a woman and as neither a fish nor a woman. Even without a stitch or scar visible between her two halves, it is implied there has been a separation and then a unification. In *The Dreaded Comparison*, Marjorie Spiegel writes about the connections between human-to-human violence and human-to-animal violence. She explains that the violence White people (often men considered to be gentlemen) inflict/ed on nonhuman animals and the violence they inflict/ed on Black and Indigenous people is how they succeed/ed at dehumanization. "Because society's opinion of animals was so low," Spiegel writes about early nineteenth-century American literature, "racist authors and anti-abolitionists propagandized against blacks by comparing them to negative stereotypes of non-human animals... imbued with none of the respect with which Native Americans gave to the use of animal names."[5]

Photos and drawings appear throughout Spiegel's book, side-by-side visual aids illustrating how similar objects of restraint and similar language have been used to dominate or devalue both people and animals. In one such juxtaposition, a photo of a Black enslaved woman holding a chubby White baby is placed opposite a photo of veal calves chained to their stalls, separated from their mothers. Unspoken are understandings of confinement, forbidden and thwarted motherhood, and bodies as food.

Spiegel explains that this violence stems from fear and denial. "People who dislike or are afraid of elements within themselves, such as strong emotion, sexual feelings, weakness, or violent urges, repress even their own knowledge of these parts of themselves... fear of the so-called 'irritational' part of one's own self. People deny these elements, yet at the same time want or need to know them, so they are projected onto someone or something else: women, black people, Jews, animals, of even Nature itself."[6] These projections are a result of internal conflict; a simmering happens beneath the skin and explodes in violence. Nowhere does Spiegel blame a mother.

Perhaps I shouldn't either. Once, I questioned whether Jim and Wes's behavior could be traced back to the stories I'd heard about their mother. How perhaps she instigated the removal of her husband from their home, how there might have been something fishy about her relationship with Jim. But those stories remain as stories. They cannot be verified; their mother is dead. An absent referent. I don't want to blame a mother, that feels too easy, too full of misogyny. Too close to home. If I blame her, I am no better than they are, two strangers judging my mothering. The brothers were the ones at fault, adult men making choices, acting intentionally, a disregard for our privacy, our sense of safety. I fear what they might have recognized in me.

◎ ◎ ◎

Maggie Nelson writes in *The Art of Cruelty* that we want to hurt ourselves as much as we want to hurt others. This parallels with Spiegel's claims, and I wonder if this explains my relationship with Wes and Jim. Did they want to harm themselves as much as they harmed us? Could they have wanted to force us from our home because they feared their own? Sometimes, back then and even now, when I remember something I did or said, something that was mean or embarrassing, I feel a sharp pain inside, near my lungs. Sometimes, when the thing remembered is especially sharp, I imagine pressing a knife between my ribs, horizontally to miss the bones, to stab at the soft spot where I feel the harm. Could the brothers, too, have felt that thing, that wet regret?

I don't think so. Wes hurled accusations at me, but his was not the first or only voice to express those kinds of denouncements.

Political candidates and radio hosts and Twitter bots with cartoon avatars all accuse me and other women like me of neglect: A good mother cannot be divorced, a single mom, a remarried mom. A working mom, a mom in graduate school, an artist mom. Those kinds of moms are careless, selfish. Notice, though, how all these assertions subtract *woman* and use only the word *mom*, as if the two could not be the same. Fish or woman, but not both.

And still, while the brothers followed us, closed me in my car, yelled, spied, and pried, I felt I had put my son in harm's way, moving into this house, even if I couldn't have known. Because once in, we couldn't get out. So I fixated instead on how to stop them. Sacks of oranges, icy driveways, an accidental reverse in my car. Nelson's argument about harm gets close to what I think I am searching for, not just in explaining the motivations behind Jim and Wes's behavior, but as a way to understand my reactions to them. Before them, I had never wished so much for someone else to, if not die, then be gone. I wanted to hurt them. That want grew from the pit in my stomach, fed on the fear and shame I felt about being incapable of protecting my child. And what greater fear is that? What greater failure could there be?

◉ ◉ ◉

Nelson also writes of our relationship to death, our own and the deaths of others, as an interest in becoming not a dead *person*, but something else. "The spectre of our eventual 'becoming object'—of our (live) flesh one day turning into (dead) meat—is a shadow that accompanies us throughout our lives."[7] Death's shadow presence is the reason we hedge our bets, why we proceed with caution. For most, death's presence, and our fear of it, creates a desire for self-preservation. I do not want to be dead (meat). This is why the metaphor "I felt like dead meat" is so evocative, so effective. The phrase is, I think, less a doubling of animal harm, as Carol J. Adams claims, and linked more to inevitability. Like Despentes telling us not to think about "if a rape occurs," but rather "when a rape occurs," I think saying Wes's stares "made me feel like dead meat" feels accurate because I was thinking not about *if* he would harm me, but *when*. In the thick of their crusade to push us out of this house, an escalation to physical harm felt as inevitable as death.[8]

Magritte's fish woman repels me because of her nearness to death, how she reminds me of my own mortality, of my own object-ness. But I am drawn to her because she embodies crossed bound-aries, and mine have been crossed and I have crossed them. I love her naked vulnerability. She has been cultivated into something new via acts of brutality and reconstruction. She is familiar and strange simultaneously, attractive and abject, violent and erotic. I am her, and she is me. So too am I Magritte, making art from what confuses me, hurts me, hurts those I love. I look at *Collective Invention* and I recognize the feeling of being both home and not home, halfway out of my element, gasping for breath and unable to run.

◉ ◉ ◉

I am certain now that it was me who shouted *Fuck off, Wes* that summer night we tried to camp in the yard. I know that my hus-band would not have said it, not in front of our child, and likely not ever, not loudly, because he does not swear as often as I swear. "Speech of this kind—" writes Michael Adams in *In Praise of Profanity*, "is the violent expression of emotion, though violence miniaturized and concentrated in the mouth."[9] I like this idea of a miniaturized and concentrated anger, as if I could take in all that made me want to hurt them and chew it into a wad.

Weeks later, in the driveway, as I got into the car again without saying hello to Jim and Wes, I did it once more. They were walk-ing quickly toward the fence, yelling about my rude insistence on ignoring them *once again*, that I'd *never learn*. I muttered *Fuck off*, just loud enough for them to hear. They stopped, stared. And then Wes said, *Such language out of a lady. Such language in front of your child! A child should not hear that kind of talk. A woman like you shouldn't have kids. I'm going to call the authorities. I'm going to report you and they'll take your son away. I know people. I worked for the biggest city in the world. I sued them, you know. I beat them. I'm so rich I don't need to work, but I still know people there. And they love me. They'll want to help me.*

Fuck is a word that we use for sex, perhaps especially rough sex, and it is also a word we use in anger. *Fuck* is the opposite of gentle. We use it when we feel something swell inside, a way to articulate the anger we chew on; *fuck* is the bolus of rage we spit out like a spitball. *Fuck* is a word we are taught is wrong and so we feel compelled to use it when we are being wronged. Michael Adams says one of the reasons we use words like this is because "extraordinary events call for extraordinary measures."[10] For three years, Wes and Jim followed me, watched us over the fence and through our windows. There can be eroticism to looking, but when that looking is not consensual, it becomes an act of violence. Remember the voice of the man in the car, the *Fuck you Wes* that hit all the windows in the neighborhood that summer night? I am certain that shout was a release for that man, because it was for me. Spitting, too, is uncouth. To say *Fuck off* then seems to me to be the most accurate response to their behavior.

I told Wes to fuck off and then we got in the car and drove away. I didn't understand his claims about lawsuits and connections and "knowing people." Confused, I looked it up when I got home, found a newspaper article in a paper known for being dubious.[11] Still, this meant he'd told the truth. I was terrified he would call. I was, at that time, restructuring the custody agreement I had with my ex-husband.

If he called, no one followed up. Likely it was an empty threat, he was faking me out, all this a game to him, one where he found endless ways to keep me on edge. But just to be sure, I did not shout *Fuck off* at him again.

Duck: v. To avoid getting hit.
    Often yelled as a warning.
    (See also *chicken*.)

Maybe I interpreted Magritte's fish woman as a depiction of his mother's death because I know the feeling of being trapped by a man, or because I also know the gasping desperation of motherhood. Maybe I saw her as an amalgamation of sex and death because I have swallowed misogyny like microplastics, feel shame about my body. But what if there is another way to read this image?

What if Magritte's fish woman, or my sculpture of his fish woman, is instead seen as an undoing of the hierarchy of human animal over nonhuman animal? In a gentler reading, there is a symbiosis. Land and sea, human and animal. The power to run and the ability to live underwater. Mother and sex and death and breath and water. My sculpture of her fits on my palm, heavier than she looks, and fuller. Someone has taken care to give her a second eye, another fin, a soft bottom, and tender knee hollows.

IX. On paranoia and revenge

to crow

THE WINTER-TURNED-SPRING WHEN MY FAMILY, LIKE so many others, kept inside to prevent the spread of COVID, spotted lanternflies multiplied outside. We are supposed to kill them even though their lives here are not their fault. They arrived in the US from China in 2012, along with a shipment of stone, and have since spread up and out across the eastern states. They have no natural predators, though plenty to eat, and so can decimate large numbers of trees. Every action has an equal and opposite reaction.[1]

The first time I saw one it was on a tree in front of the old hat factory down the street. We were taking a masked walk. Its feverish wings caught my eye. I took off my shoe and smashed it. Before I did it, though, and even after, I looked around to see if anyone had seen me. Killing it felt wrong and I did not want our neighbors to know what I'd done. Shame is a feeling tied to looking, to the heat that rises after being caught by another. In *Being and Nothingness*, Sartre writes about a man looking through a peephole, about being seen watching: "I see myself because somebody sees me." Even though I knew it was impossible, I swore I could feel the small lump of the lanternfly's broken body underfoot for the remainder of my walk, reminding me what I'd done, like the beating heart beneath the floorboards in Poe's "The Tell-Tale Heart."

Though there is a sidewalk in front of our house now, there wasn't always. Before the city's initiative to make this part of town more walkable, the patchy grass of our front yard scrubbed its way around the pine and the dogwood for a few feet and then became street. This means whenever Wes and Jim dumped their leaves in the parking lot of the condominiums at the end of the road, they walked through our yard to do so. The night Wes leaned on our fence and (shamelessly) shined his flashlight in our tent, he was even deeper into our space. Although Matt succeeded in convincing Wes to back up, he did not back off. He did not go home. Wes stayed on the grass where a sidewalk may have been, where one exists now. That night, like all the times he'd walked through before, Wes preached that the first three feet of any property, whether sidewalked or not, belong to the city, therefore making it public property. He could stand there if he wanted to. It was his right.

When we arrived for our first appointment to walk through this house, after we had looked at the other three and deemed them unsuitable, there were small pink begonias planted around the trees. Jerry's chairs rocked at perfect angles on the front porch. We did not think to be concerned about a sidewalk, did not think people walking through our yard could be anything less than neighborly, anything more than none of our business. We imagined sitting in our own rocking chairs, barefooted and drinking coffee, waving at new neighbors.

During the years we lived beside Jim and Wes, if we did sit on the porch at all our vigilant eyes remained on the driveway. And if they pulled in while we were sitting, we shrunk back inside, careful not to let the door slam so as not to be noticed.

◉ ◉ ◉

I had finished graduate school a few weeks prior to the night Wes disrupted our attempt at backyard camping. We were looking forward to the changes fall would bring, not just in the trees and the weather, but come September, I would be adjuncting at a different school and our son would start third grade. The reason backyard camping had seemed so necessary is our near-third grader had been wanting to hang out with us less, had recently started the slow pull toward independence by choosing to play more with his friends. Whenever he went out the back door to meet them, I reminded him to keep an eye out for the neighbors. *Just in case*, I said. *And if they pull up, it's probably nothing, but you should play inside instead.* Was this an attempt to tourniquet my fears so they did not become his, or a necessary warning about the possibility of a confrontation—or the possibility of something worse? Upstairs, the shade on my son's bedroom window stays closed.

◎ ◎ ◎

In a last-ditch effort to unchoke the garden before summer ends, I yanked hard on some tree of heaven pushing through the daylilies. Beneath a leaf, a small black and red beetle shaped like an aardvark. I took a picture but left him where he stood, his sticky feet against the smooth stem. Then I carefully brought him back to the compost. I even apologized to him for the interruption. I went inside, washed my hands, then googled *red-and-black-beetle-with-white-spots.* I had relocated a spotted lanternfly nymph. Back outside, I tried to find it, crush it, but it was gone. I am tempted to correct my pronoun slip above, my switch from *him* to *it.* But this is how I know I wanted so badly to distance myself from my role in death. I turned the living bug into an object. Killing a *who* demands something different than killing an *it.*[2]

I did not find the nymph. But days later I saw one on the cherry tree near the kitchen window. Holding my breath, I flicked it to the ground. Then I placed a brick on top and walked away.

The brick is still there. It is possible the nymph crawled away, an escape by way of some gap between the brick and the ground. If not, if I crushed the nymph, then I have done what was expected of me. Eve Kosofsky Sedgwick says, "shame can be seen as good because it preserves privacy and decency, bad because it colludes with self-repression or social repression."[3] I am ashamed of my violent act because it feels indecent, as it should. But this shame also makes me want to avoid dealing with these thoughts at all. If I refuse to turn over the brick, the not-knowing assuages my shame. Schrödinger's nymph.

◎ ◎ ◎

I do not know what day it was, but I do remember Matt was at work and it wasn't the brothers' usual day to pick up leaves or get the mail. My son and I were going to take the dog for a walk, or we were going to ride our bikes, or we were running an errand. He walked out of the front door before me, and I heard Wes's voice. The repetition and the echo rang clear even when his words were indecipherable.

They had parked their car in our driveway, on our side of the fence. They were standing between the front of their car and the back of ours, looking into my backseat, hands cupped around their eyes and pressed against the windows. I stood on the front porch, told my son to get back inside and close the door. I yelled, *Get off my car.* Wes straightened his posture. Did he smile? He asked how long my son had been playing soccer. He didn't play soccer anymore, and it was late March, but there was still a pair of muddy cleats in the car. I yelled again, louder, and did not stop yelling as they walked closer. First I yelled for them to get away from my car, then to get out of my driveway, and then I yelled that I was calling the police. When I pulled my phone from my pocket, Jim laughed. Wes said, *Don't you film me.* I knew that my anger was pointless, that calling the police would likely lead nowhere. What is that threat but an empty cup? And yet. I called anyway, and when someone answered I leveled my voice so as not to be thought hysterical, to be taken seriously. I said, *My neighbors have blocked me in my driveway and are refusing to leave.*

All they had wanted for the last three years was for us to leave this house. And now they were blocking us in.

I want you to remember this from Despentes's essay: "I wish I'd been able to escape the values instilled in my gender that night, and slit each of their throats, one by one. Instead of having to live with being someone who didn't dare defend herself, because she's a woman and violence is not her domain, and the physical integrity of the male body is more important than that of the female."[4] A pressure grew in my head so great I felt as if my eyes would fall out. I felt that I could, in that moment, follow through on years of fantasies (sacks of oranges, a car in reverse). But I knew I could only do what was expected of me. I did not leave the porch. On the phone, I was polite to the police.

After hanging up, I looked at them still in my driveway, shouted *See? See?* I do not know exactly what I wanted them to see, except that I had followed through on my threat. For years, Wes and Jim had accused me of being a bad mother, had stared, trespassed, threatened, held me in my car, looked through my trash, followed us to work, to the grocery store. Once, we went to vote at the elementary school near the city dump and there they were, volunteers in matching red hats. All acts of intimidation. But they had never followed through. Wes moved from the driveway to the front of my house. He stood in the spot where our cracked walkway met the street and paced in a small circle. I did not leave the porch, just watched him out in the open, his brother, too, looking at me and then Wes, until the police arrived. One car, lights spinning red and blue. Two officers stepped out.

◉ ◉ ◉

And then Wes fell to the ground.

◎ ◎ ◎

I had wanted them gone for so long, had wanted them to stop fol-
lowing/looking/trapping/shouting. But then Wes was flat on his
back, his feet pointing up as if his heels were sinking into a fis-
sure in our walkway. It could not have been quiet, there must have
been shouts from Jim or the officers, there must have been traffic or
walkie-talkie static or dogs barking, but I only remember stillness,
silence, and tunnel vision. "Staring, in its pure and simple essence,"
writes Jeanne McDermott, "is the time required by the brain to
make sense of the unexpected."[5]

◎ ◎ ◎

Because almost anything can remind me of Wes and Jim, when
I first wrote about the spotted lanternflies, I thought I saw a parallel between the insects' invasiveness and our boundary-crossing
neighbors, between my bug-crushing and my attic-desires to hurt
Jim and Wes. But the metaphor fell apart. Their invasion of our
space, of our privacy, of our sense of safety was an intentional act
of harm, power, and control. The spotted lanternflies arrived via
cargo ship. They are here by accident and circumstance, merely
looking for food, a place to land, to perpetuate their species. I am
more like the lanternfly.

◎ ◎ ◎

I can't get to the truest story of the neighbors without aligning
them, or what happened, with something else, something not-
them. I turned to lanternflies like I turned to rhinos, poems,
horseshoe crabs, performance art, bug collections, elephants, horror films, and art. Like I turned to animal verb etymologies. I am
looking wherever I can for reasons. The rhinos, poems, horseshoe
crabs, performance art, bug collections, elephants, horror films,
and art function as metaphors do—comparisons getting closer to
what I can't get to otherwise. And then, as I work to comprehend

the brothers' actions, I understand them as part of something larger, though seeing them as symbolic of settler colonialism seems more literal. Their behavior was both unlike anything I had seen before and exactly like everything I have seen before.

We utter about one metaphor for every ten to twenty-five words, or about six metaphors a minute.[6] Carol J. Adams argued that animal metaphors are harmful to animals, but I think when we use animals in our language, we not erasing the animal, but becoming more aware of our place in the world, more aware of how we exist in relation to them.

A metaphor is a small story. There is tension between the description and the descriptor, there are often characters and setting. You may understand something by the end of a metaphor that you didn't know before. And stories, not only those in metaphor, but also in folktales and gossip, get told repeatedly and become part of culture—they shape the way we use language to describe and discern the world. Storytelling as sense-making is universal. Anansi the Spider, The Tortoise and the Hare, The Monkey and the Crocodile, all stories told with and about animals to explain the world.[7] Even "The Tell-Tale Heart" leans into this tradition, if we think about the way Poe's narrator describes the cataracted blue eye of the victim, which was, to the murderer, a sure sign of evil and his motive for murder. (His cataract marking him Other, his murder a persecution linked to disability). "I think it was his eye! yes, it was this! One of his eyes *resembled that of a vulture*—a pale blue eye, with a film over it. Whenever it fell upon me, my blood ran cold; and so by degrees—very gradually—I made up my mind to take the life of the old man, and thus rid myself of the eye forever."[8] The vulture metaphor works twice, as these are birds that eat death and we also use their name to describe predatory people.

And Upton Sinclair's *The Jungle,* which earlier helped me think through vegetarianism, meat, women's bodies, and motherhood, is also a story filled with animals that become both metaphor and metonym. Sinclair uses animals as parallels or replacements to describe not only the violence inside the slaughterhouse, but also his characters. Look at how he describes Jurgis: When he attacks the man who raped his wife, Sinclair writes, "He fought *like a tiger*, writhing and twisting, half flinging them off, and starting toward his unconscious enemy."[9] We see him, lithe and strong, a force of brute strength fighting the men trying to subdue his rage. However, this scene ends with Jurgis being overcome: "In the end, by their sheer weight, they choked the breath out of him, and then they carried him to the company police station, where he lay still until they had summoned a patrol wagon to take him away." Captive and imprisoned, the tiger still no match for the power of man or state.

How different this scene would be if Jurgis were merely a man overtaken by men. How much higher are the stakes, now that Jurgis is tiger-like? How much stronger are those who overtake him? This isn't just about Jurgis, but about the power exerted by the state against both animals and immigrants.

◎ ◎ ◎

I think what rendered me still and speechless when I looked at Wes's crumpled form on the ground in front of my house, where my child was still inside, where I had anticipated a new life filled with calmness and laughter and new beginnings, was that Wes suddenly became nothing more than a man. I can make him into a representation of all the problems of white patriarchal colonialism, can see how he is emblematic of a long history of violence, but he was not just a representation, he is real. Prone on the cracked concrete he became fallible, soft, in a way that what he represents will never.

An ambulance came and parked in front of the police car, blocking Wes's body from the view of the street. Paramedics lifted him, gently, onto a stretcher, strapped him in, and covered him with a blanket. Before they fastened the oxygen mask to his face, he began to shout. He threatened to sue us. I had scared him, he kept saying, my yelling scared him so much he tripped on the cracked sidewalk. *I kept telling them to fix that*, he said, *and now I am having a heart attack.*

Crow: v. To utter the loud cry of a cock, to utter a loud inarticulate sound of joy or exultation; said especially of the joyful cry of an infant. To speak in exultation; to exult loudly, boast, swagger. To crow over, to triumph over. This is a shout of conquest.

Crows gather around their dead, an act that looks like mourning. Perhaps it is, though scientists believe they are actually trying to assess what happened in order to avoid the same fate. Crows do not want to die.

The ambulance drove away. One officer stayed outside with Jim, a younger one came into our house through the front door. He made a comment about all the Legos on the floor as he stood in front of where I sat on the couch, his gun and his crotch at my eye level. When the narrator in "The Tell-Tale Heart" kills his neighbor, he dismembers him and hides the pieces of his body beneath his floorboards. At the end of the story, with the police in his home, the narrator is convinced at first that his good manners will save him from getting caught. But his paranoia becomes too much and he comes clean. "I pointed at the boards and cried, 'Yes! Yes, I killed him. Pull up the boards and you shall see!'" I almost apologized, confessed to wanting Wes to die, to planning ways to harm them. The officer in my living room said he did not think Wes had a heart attack at all. That surely, we'd be fine. He wrote notes in a small notebook, wished us a good evening, and left.

I called my husband, exhausted and full of disbelief. I explained what happened and he packed his things to come home. In the two and a half hours it took him to get home, I paced from room to room and waited for guilt or relief. Instead, paranoia bloomed. I kept looking out the window for Wes to come back, or for Jim to knock and push his way in. It was starting to get dark outside. When Matt came home I told the story again, pausing when he asked questions. How did he fall? What did Jim do? How long before the police arrived? Several times he asked what our child saw, what he thought, and I couldn't know for sure. By my third retelling, the story became not just mine, but ours. The sharing did not bring either of us any sense of relief. Instead, a shared worry developed about Wes's promise to call a lawyer.

◎ ◎ ◎

My paranoia was that as defined by Eve Kosofsky Sedgwick: "anticipatory, reflexive and mimetic."[10] Every car door, every man's voice outside, every baseball hat, every unfamiliar piece of mail became a possibility of their return or a summons or a court date. I didn't even know if he had any grounds to sue us, but we had so much to lose that even the possibility sent my thoughts spiraling. It seemed impossible to move forward. Even now, as I write, I resee my house as it was back then. The door we painted yellow last summer returns to red. The hostas, toad lily, and ferns we planted out front shrivel away and return to pachysandra. The walnut tree that fell during a storm in 2020 regrows because not every memory is awful. Sometimes I ask my husband to fill in details I've forgotten, and as he tells me, and the return to memory sounds like static, my eardrums feel like they might pop. "Perhaps this pressurized orientation to memory—" writes Billy-Ray Belcourt, "one by which we understand the past as a trace that pulsates in a body in the present—is always the case with life-writing."[11]

◉ ◉ ◉

Three days after Wes collapsed out front, we heard from a neighbor who knew someone at the hospital that Wes did not have a heart attack. It was a ruse. A lie. A terrible attempt to frighten me, to get revenge, to avoid a police confrontation or arrest. Then Jim came back a few days later, but quietly. He did not look our way or shout into our windows. He parked in his own driveway, closed the car door only once, and went inside for several silent hours. Then he drove away. I watched not from the attic, but from the living room.

◉ ◉ ◉

Wes had always been the more overt, the more outspoken provocateur. He was more obvious about wanting to scare us, clearer about how he wanted to own our house. It was his hands pressed against my car window, his voice shouting about my rudeness and my ineffectual mothering. Jim pushed the lawnmower into our yard, but Wes lifted the lid on the compost bin. It was Wes on the train, Wes yelling homophobic taunts at my husband. In nearly every altercation, Jim is present, though stalwartly in the background. But a witness doesn't get to claim innocence. He must shoulder responsibility, too. Remember, the power of perpetuated systems of oppression relies on fear, but that fear must also be witnessed. Now I wonder if Jim was scared of Wes, too.

◉ ◉ ◉

Weeks passed. I stayed vigilant, worrying when the mail came, when I heard a rumbling car or saw a silver Buick, jumping when the phone rang. But no lawyers called or mailed, and neither brother visited the house. It began to get warm outside. Then Heather, who lives on the other side of the brothers, sent me a text. *Have you heard?* she asked. *Jim died. He's dead.* I called her. She said he was at work. She said, *It was his heart.*

There are questions I have no business asking. Did Jim clutch his arm? Did he know what was happening? Did he think of his brother, faking the heart attack in front of my house, and if he did, did he blame him? Was his very last thought one of assigning fault, wishing he had been better, stepped in, spoken up?

Other neighbors went to the funeral home together. We did not go, did not send flowers or a card. We stayed home, this death still not bringing any feeling of relief. I felt on edge. Here is Simone de Beauvoir, from the end of her book on losing her mother. "There is no such thing as a natural death: nothing that happens to a man is ever natural, since his presence calls the world into question."[12]

Not only their presence, but their absence. The first fall after we lost the walnut tree in the backyard to a windstorm, the remaining tree dropped more nuts than ever before. Each thud against the meat-wet ground a lament of grief and hope for regrowth.

X. On continuation

to ferret/to leech

THE SUMMER AFTER JIM'S DEATH, WE HEARD SCREAMS outside our bedroom window. Sharp and high, they woke us up in the middle of the night. I mentioned the screams to a neighbor who seemed to know more about local wildlife than we do. *I bet it's a fisher cat*, he said. Fisher cats are members of the weasel family. They are shy, have thick, dark fur, and eat small rodents. The screaming worried me at first, but then I remembered that young man's voice, the one who drove by and screamed *Fuck you Wes* from his car. A scream can be a purge.

It turns out we were wrong. Fisher cats don't scream at all. More likely it was a fox, which we had seen a few times before, once in our yard, flinging a left-behind dog toy. The rabbit population in our neighborhood decreased that summer. Lucky for the gardeners, not so lucky for the rabbits.

You don't see them much anymore, but when I was a kid, you could buy a rabbit's foot attached to a silver chain. Sometimes their fur was dyed an unnatural color, and beneath the bright softness you could feel the rabbit's brittle bones and claws. People attached them to their key chains or kept them hidden in their pockets, a talisman to be petted or touched for good luck.

Ferret: v. First used to mean to hunt with ferrets. By the seventeenth century *to ferret* also meant to worry after. Or to drive away. A few decades earlier we see it used the way we do now, meaning to rummage or tease something out, but also to be restless with worry. It also appears that once, in 1699, ferreted meant cheated.

Ferrets were domesticated 2,500 years ago and used to hunt rabbits.

A coat made of ferret fur is called *fitch*, which seems like a way to make its skinning anonymous. A coat made of rabbit is still called rabbit. They have never been used to hunt anything.

Carrying a rabbit's foot as a good luck charm stretches back to the late eighteenth century, where it was originally an African American tradition believed to subvert conventional power structures like the White police force. At that same time, White people, who associated rabbits with the uncanny, also began holding the dismembered feet to ward off evil. Much of the rabbit's foot lore revolves around the capturing and killing of the rabbit itself. Frequently, it was said that the rabbit should be killed in a cemetery (by whom and with what changed quite a bit and became often paradoxical and ludicrously complicated) and so, the rabbits' capacity to challenge power structures was associated with death and dismemberment. When writing about this tradition and noting its spike in popularity in the late nineteenth century, Bill Ellis notes "...it was assimilated into white culture at the very moment when lynchings were rapidly becoming more and more politically risky." No longer able to keep the desecrated body parts of Black people they lynched as souvenirs, they pocketed rabbits' feet instead.

Stuart Vyse traces a Westernized lexical and practical history of superstition from the fourth century BCE in Greece up through Europe and North. The word's Latin roots mean "to stand over," as in, "to stand over something in awe."

Superstition has always been used to describe practices that fall outside of more traditional worldviews, especially when those practices fall beyond the parameters of elite citizens' religious practices. Later, the Romans discounted the superstitious as unserious people "surrendering to fear and passion," whose beliefs and practices "conflicted with the ordered sense of the universe."[1] An order established, of course, by those with status.

By the first century CE, all practices outside of Roman religions were disregarded as superstitions and this thinking stuck. Hundreds of years later, the Christians of the fifteenth century deemed the practice of witchcraft heretical, demanding all witches killed. These same Christians began the tradition of coding witches as female, claiming "witches were more often women because their deficient intellect made them more vulnerable...and women were prone to the extremes of good and evil." Superstitions, then, are not only deadly but gendered.[2]

The superstitious people whose beliefs and practices fell outside the confines of elite, patriarchal religious traditions were excluded from that patriarchal, religious, traditional society, a form of exile. This practice followed the Europeans to the Americas. First, they rejected the Indigenous practices of those who already lived here, and then the African faiths held by the enslaved people they forced here. Then, as is seen with the rabbit's foot, they appropriated it. Superstition is used as a tool, a colonial strategy of subjugation that made division by belief seem logical. The "superstitious (whether that exact word is used or not) are somehow less than full citizens, less than equal participants in the projects of the secular state." Superstitions are part of culture, rooted in believing that it is possible to ward off what can potentially harm. But when they are tied to the magical and the paranormal, to women and people of color, they are discredited.

◎ ◎ ◎

Anytime she was in a car, my college roommate performed a ritual hand gesture when she saw a yellow Ryder moving van on the highway. She licked her right thumb and dragged it across her left palm, snapped her fingers, then hit her right fist against her open left palm. She also kissed her first three fingers and touched them to the car ceiling whenever we went through a yellow light. These acts were meant to keep us safe from accidents. I understood these potential dangers well, so it wasn't long before I performed them, too. Still do.

Two years before I met my superstitious roommate, when I was a junior in high school, two boys in the class ahead of me died in separate car accidents, the first in a drag race. The second, a boy I loved the way you do when you are sixteen, uncontrollably, sat on the roof of a car on his way to a party, his feet dangling inside the sunroof, and then he fell off. The tragedies of young people are often felt as both personal and collective griefs, though mine, ours, was also mixed with something like relief. For the seven consecutive years prior to these deaths, a graduating senior from our school died. When Robbie fell off the roof of that car, the ninth in our tragic timeline, someone from the *New York Times* wrote an article about our curse.[3] (The journalist does not call it a curse.

He calls it a "misplaced disbelief in mortality," though having attended so many funerals, I am certain we more than believed in our own mortality.) In it, his mom names his death as suicide induced by drug and alcohol abuse rather than the result of reckless teen behavior. She was friends with my mother, and when I first read what she'd said I'd found her statement cold.

For the entirety of my senior year, we all held our breath driving past graveyards, crossed our fingers whenever someone mentioned our curse. Superstition as protection. But by June we were still as many as we were in September. Curse broken. A history is a record of the past. A legacy is what defines that past.

"If judgment is our faculty for dealing with the past, the historian is the inquiring man who by relating it sits in judgment over it," writes Hannah Arendt in *Postscriptum to Thinking*. Retelling the past requires a series of interpretations, all biased and changeable over time. Humans seem to be uniquely able to imagine alternate possibilities, including, as I read in Thomas Suddendorf's *The Gap*, worst-case scenarios. It is this ability, I think, that leads us to be superstitious (or religious) in the first place. The first time we heard the fox screaming outside our window, I thought a woman was being murdered.

⊚ ⊚ ⊚

We did not go to Jim's funeral for the same reason we did not move the gargoyle statue left behind in our backyard, the one the brothers claimed to have given to the previous owner of our house. An unsubstantiated fear that if we did, something worse would happen. Not to mention that going to Jim's funeral seemed inappropriate, like an act of curiosity rather than one of grief. But not going also brought about a churning in my stomach. Guilt and relief and the guilt of feeling relief. I am remembering now, again, Camille Dungy's *Guidebook to Relative Strangers*, though not the chapter about the grieving mothers on the *Brooklyn*. Further in the book, she writes about the destruction of her hometown, a destruction made in the name of construction, of progress. "When I write about nature, I write about loss," she says, and I think about how a place, like a person, can be a reminder.

We did not go to the funeral but we heard about it from other neighbors who did. They said Wes was there in a wheelchair, a blanket over his lap, his face thin and unshaven. He had jumped from a height high enough to break both of his legs. I don't know anything more but cannot shake the image of him on our cracked sidewalk, as if that entire night was a precursor to his brother's fate, a jinx. "Life," Foucault said, "it seems is quite fragile in the human species and death quite certain."[4] If I close my eyes, I can still conjure the shape of Wes's chin.

I know I wasn't the cause of Jim's death, and that Wes's faked heart attack had nothing to do with his brother's real one, but still, I feel a twinge of self-centered responsibility. Thinking something does not make it so, but I can't help but trace our steps backward: Wes's jump, Jim's death, Wes's faked heart attack, my yelling, my daydreams of harm, their ceaseless threatening presence, our move to this house. I know I am not responsible, but shame returns, hot and familiar. "Shame illuminates our intense attachment to the world, our desire to be connected with others, and the knowledge that, as merely human, we will sometimes fail in our attempts to maintain those connections,"[5] says Elspeth Probyn in *Blush: Faces of Shame*. Merely human. Should I have tried harder, been kinder? Or disengaged entirely? Or moved? What am I ashamed of? My actions, or my inactions?

◎ ◎ ◎

In the fall of 2023, I taught a writing class on hybrid forms as political resistance. We read Claudia Rankine's *Don't Let Me Be Lonely* and then, a few weeks later, we met up in New Haven to see her read at Yale's Beinecke Library, where a collection of protest art was being displayed on both floors. In my office, before we left, I thumbed through Rankine's pages again, stopping at the Post-it note I'd stuck on page forty-eight. This is where she writes against Derrida's assertion that forgiveness is a form of madness. She says instead, "For the one who forgives, it is simply a death, a dying down in the heart, the position of the already dead. It is in the end the living through, the understanding that this has happened, is happening, happens. Period." Living beside them had once been a source of worry, shame, anger, and guilt. Then, so quickly, became...nothing. At first a legacy and then a history. Alive and then dead. I had not thought a forgiveness possible or even necessary, but to think of forgiveness as Rankine does—a dying down in the heart—meant forgiving the brothers did not mean closure. A dying down is a quieting, not a silencing. What the brothers represent is still happening, still happens. Actually, I don't think I need to concern myself with forgiveness at all. I need to focus instead on what it means to live a life that is gentle.

◎ ◎ ◎

I tell my students that writing nonfiction is a pushing through, like giving birth: Hindsight gives way to insight. I warn them that this does not mean they will find goodness where a hurt once was, that sometimes it happens the other way around. A hurt might become a meadow. But just as easily, a hope can turn into an earthquake.

Here's the thing about the years we spent living next to Jim and Wes—even when focused elsewhere, their presence seeped into my thoughts. So, like my switch to vegetarianism, my graduate school thesis ideas seem also to have been unconsciously neighbor-related. Earlier, I thought my wavering between late nineteenth century American novels and performance art was a consequence of balancing motherhood and school. I thought that I leaned into performance art because I was acting in two different roles, mother/student, and because I was trying to find the meaning of my body.

I ignored, until now, how much that interest came from knowing I was being watched.

Leech: v. At one time *to leech* meant to heal, to cure, because we used leeches to drain the bad out of blood; we used them on our bodies because we believed they could help us remove the toxins that ailed us. *To leech* someone was to care about their well-being. We stopped believing in the leech as a tool for healing in the late nineteenth century and now we only use *to leech* when we mean to latch on, like a parasite. To be parasitic.

◎ ◎ ◎

Months ago, while working on this book, I sat on our couch to reread Upton Sinclair's *The Jungle* preparing to write about vegetarianism and horror movies, meat and women's bodies. I chose the couch because it felt important to be as comfortable as possible while I worked on something uncomfortable. In fact, I have written this entire manuscript sitting on couches or lying in bed, never at a desk or in a dining room chair. In between the pages of *The Jungle*, I found my ten-year-old notes about Social Darwinism and Naturalism scribbled on notecards. So many of the books published during this period of American history depict poverty as a failure of the individual, while also justifying society's racism, imperialism, and conservatism by applying a misunderstanding of survival of the fittest. At the time I wrote these notecards, I thought I was researching the disdain these novels had for women and children. But this was just another way to understand the consequences of aggressive masculinity in my country and on my street.

Sometimes a superstition is not a ritual act, but a ritual thought. As a mother, I have spent too much time picturing worst-case scenarios. My son falling out of cars, from ferris wheels, off hiking trails or bikes. School shootings, predators, perverts. I have dreamed or imagined these scenarios in an attempt to ward them off, as if imagination is a form of prevention. I try to prevent my own death this way, too, to stave off the grief my son would feel if he had to outlive me. I avoid heights, highway on-ramps with low visibility, and dark parking lots. I never swim out too far. "She is frightened of her children, because now that they've arrived in the world she has to stay here for as long as she can but not longer than they do,"[6] writes Lauren Groff in "Flower Hunters." Motherhood is always connected to death.

Magritte, Dungy, de Beauvoir. Cassie from *The Book of X* and Ona from *The Jungle*. The mother of my dead high school friend. Why do I keep returning to mother grief when writing about Wes and Jim? Because of all the ways motherhood is connected to violence. The pain of labor, the fear of heartbreak, the endless acceptance of uncertainty. The powerlessness of mothers within a country where birth is considered by some to be our duty, though health care and childcare remain too often out of reach. I wanted to hurt those two men. I wanted to protect my son.

They should not have followed us, mowed our lawn, rifled through our compost, stolen the survey stick, dumped yard debris onto shared space, hollered at me, my husband, my mother, trapped me in my car, shone a flashlight into our yard, or watched us over the fence. No one would consider the brothers "good people." But more than anger over breached boundaries or misplaced claims on the house we live in, for the years we lived beside the brothers I felt fear and shame on a constant loop. Wes tried to emasculate my husband by questioning his sexuality. However, when he insulted me, he attacked my ability to mother well. A prod into my darkest fear. Could he have known this was also how I most frequently chastised myself? And Jim, with his watching, more aloof than his outspoken brother, but always looking. What could he see?

◎ ◎ ◎

What if they were right? What if I failed as a mother, if I lost my son? What if he was taken away?

Though Wes's threats to report me were terrifying, my whiteness and my education meant the judges and lawyers would be less likely to scrutinize me. Indigenous scholars, like Maile Arvin, Eve Tuck, and Angie Morrill, have reminded us "having children is a privilege that has been historically denied to many nonwhite and nonaffluent people."[7] There is no record of what happened to the enslaved Nanny or her baby after the libel trial surrounding that baby's paternity closed. The poor Mormon women on the *Brooklyn* buried dozens of babies at sea. When they arrived, finally, on the coast of California that offered them new hope, they stood, "unaware, on the graves of Tuchayunes killed by overwork and European disease." In the winter of 2023, as I write this paragraph, a woman in Texas is repeatedly denied an abortion despite the fetus's fatal condition, the possibility of maternal death, and the possibility that her future pregnancies might be impossible.[8] Mother grief is as historical as it is common. I turn to it because it is something I already understand.

◎ ◎ ◎

When I was sixteen I silently accused Robbie's mother of being cold in her interview, but I remember her at the church. Her steady voice contradicted the contracting muscles in her hand. Her eyes closed a beat longer than expected, and when opened looked at all of us in rows, searching, perhaps, for her son and then remembering he wasn't there. I no longer think her response was cold. I think she had imagined the possibility of his death before. Lying awake and whispering fears into the dark. But preparation does not work as prevention.

Where do we go when all is lost?

I used to bite my son's fingernails while he nursed. At his most still, and often reaching toward my face, I could chew away his sharp edges. In a rush to leave the house on a chilly afternoon, I caught his ragged thumbnail on the cuff of his sleeve. Instead of stopping to nurse and use my teeth, I thought I could save time if I used the special infant clippers instead, the ones with the magnifying glass attached at the top. He didn't move when I held his hand in mine, didn't flinch at the metal clipper, but still, I misjudged. I clipped the thin skin of his thumb. He wailed. And then I cried, too. This was the first time his blood made contact with air. My own thumb throbbed.

Worse hurts have happened since, this was only the first. I wrapped a tiny Band-Aid around his thumb. Later I called my mother. When I was an infant, she took her eyes off me for a handful of seconds while washing clothes at a laundromat. As she did, someone else's child pushed me from the table I was sleeping on. I fell out of the car seat I was in and smacked my head against the concrete floor. It is possible to fail at protection, to be the cause of pain, even when living to prevent it.

◎ ◎ ◎

We did not go to Jim's funeral but heard from a neighbor that he is buried in a cemetery across the street from a church and next to a strip of stores and a large house recently rezoned for commerce. A few months ago, that house opened as a business that sells and installs fences. They have a huge sign out front, the kind used in road construction zones, and it flashes a slogan about making America great. In the cemetery, Jim is buried next to his mother.

◎ ◎ ◎

For two months after Jim's funeral, the yellow house remained empty. No one mowed the lawn. A younger man I'd never seen before came and got the mail. Then someone in a pickup truck pulled in the driveway and hammered a for sale sign into the front yard. It took some time, but within the year, it sold.

A dumpster arrived. Men in masks and thick gloves spent long hours and many days bringing furniture, newspapers, rugs, and piles of clothes out of the house. When one dumpster filled, it was hauled away and replaced by a new one. Eventually we heard sheetrock, tiles, and old kitchen cabinets being thrown away. It is impossible not to worry over the waste.[9]

Once the last of the trash was removed, new work began. The roof reshingled, a new garage door hung, the windows replaced, and yellow shingles torn away so gray siding could be installed. They built a small deck off the back and then flanked the windows with blue shutters. They paved their side of the driveway smooth. Often, I watched from the front porch. On the days the workmen were outside when I brought my son home from school, we smiled and waved hello.

◎ ◎ ◎

We live in a country founded on mother grief. A history of infants stolen from their enslaved and Indigenous mothers. A legacy of maternal mortality rates and unpaid maternity leave. My own mother grief comes from the sadness of something both potential and inevitable. I could lose my son in a thousand unspeakable ways. And he could lose me. I just read Sarah Manguso's interview with Kate Zambreno from a few years ago. They are talking about the impetus behind Zambreno's *Book of Mutter*, which she wrote after her mother's death. "I could not imagine the complete devastation of motherhood, and how that would make me suddenly return to the grief and the desire for the ritual of working over that grief." I imagine this grief all the time, a superstition, a devotion to devastation.

The reason I couldn't simply ignore Jim and Wes or push them from my thoughts, the reason I watched them so closely and imagined their deaths is because they had tapped into this darkest of griefs, a tapping into that only worked because they also suffered it. Magritte painted fragmented women. Barthes, after publishing the memoir where his rib piece's fate is written, wrote *Camera Lucida* to grieve the death of his mother. As far as I can tell, those brothers never changed the house they grew up in, their mother's house. They never took out anything that she'd brought in. The last thing removed once they were gone was her dust-covered car.

I need my son to love me, but not too much.

◎ ◎ ◎

But there is something more. I keep turning to mothers, even Jim and Wes's mother, to see if that's where blame belongs, though I know that that, too, is my own fear reflected back. I was the one so close to failing. We spend our whole lives trying to pull away from our mothers, to establish ourselves as individuals, as not-them. But at the same time, we feel we need to keep them near enough to look at, as if we might figure them out.

I don't know where Wes is now. He never came back. If I google him, other folks with his same name populate the page, then I scroll past the article about his lawsuit and a record of his voter registration in this city, where his address is still listed as next door. I do not wish him harm but I do not wish him well. I simply wish him to stay away. But I keep pulling his story back. He, too, a strange mother figure, tethered to what I know of myself.

◎ ◎ ◎

The reconstruction of their old house was finished in a matter of months. And then a new car pulled into the garage. Even though

I knew it couldn't be him, the sound of a door slam still startled until I looked outside. That house does not belong to the brothers anymore. But it never really did. Just like our house is not ours. Not because of unfinished mortgage payments, but because no house, no yard, no space is ever really anyone's. We are each merely temporary caregivers.

A small SUV pulled into the driveway, parked in the garage. Behind it, a moving truck. A tall White woman, with brown hair and glasses, moved her things in quickly and quietly. A few days later, she rang our doorbell, introduced herself. She was a chemist, and invited us over for wine and cheese.

◎ ◎ ◎

In *The Texas Chain Saw Massacre*, before Pam falls into the bone-filled living room, we see her as she walks up to the cannibals' house. This scene is shot from behind, her bare back exposed in a foreshadowing of her gruesome murder. But once she reaches the front porch the camera angle changes. We see Pam's face through the screen door, from inside of the house looking out, the metal decoration of the doorframe cutting across her neck. As we reached the front door of Jim and Wes's old place, I noticed the front door had been replaced. Now there is no screen door at all, only a solid gray door with a small window at the top and a Ring security camera doorbell to the left of the door handle. Matt held the wine and a bouquet of flowers for our new neighbor, so I rang the bell, my stomach inside-out with vestigial fear.

Would Wes know, somehow, that we would be here (*This is the house that was built for us*) and come back to take what he thought was his? Would he blame me for the death of his brother, the loss of his house, the removal of the lights he had so painstakingly placed around the perimeter? Would he seek revenge? What would he use as a weapon? A hook, a gun, a flowerpot? This feels like the opening of an apocalypse story, a retelling of *The Texas Chain Saw Massacre*, maybe, with two White, suburban adults about to stumble into a house that once held horrors, though perhaps I am too much inside my own head.[10] Leni answered the door, welcomed us to her new home. It smelled of lemons and cleaning products. It would be rude to turn my back and run. Inside, there was a fireplace in the living room and the wood floors reflected our feet. The light through the windows caught on the glasses she had already set out on her table, clear and open.

◎ ◎ ◎

We sat on Leni's brand-new couch and she lit a fire even though it was not cold. Everything glowed with light, and she told us how she loved to travel, how she liked to sail and was so happy to be near the sea. We told her about our son, our lives together, and soon we were laughing. She poured more wine and the sun went down. The kitchen cabinets were painted white and because the fireplace was gas powered, it made no noise. The bricks surrounding it looked older than the insert, original to the house, and I knew that the brothers likely touched those bricks, hung Christmas stockings from that mantle, or maybe, when it was a wood-burning fireplace, they stoked the flames with an iron poker.

Maybe I shouldn't have, but I started to tell Leni about the brothers, about her house that was once their house. I don't know why, except I was afraid she could sense my hesitation, my discomfort, and I didn't want her to think I was uncomfortable around her. How strange to be in their physical space when they had for so long taken up so much of my thinking. Or maybe what is strange is that I hadn't been in there before. I half expected to find evidence of what they had done to us—a picture of us tacked to the wall or a blueprint of our house unrolled across a table. But there was not a trace of their lives anywhere. I laughed as I told her how they had peered into our trash, laughed as if they had not made me feel shame and terror, as if they had not turned me into someone I wasn't. As if her fresh start could also, somehow, be mine.

I asked Leni where her bathroom was, and she told me I would see it down the hall, first door on the right. I already knew this, because from the outside I can see that window is smaller than all the others. I closed the door behind me and locked it, took in the gleaming tile and clean mirror. Her toothbrush on the edge of the sink, in a cup the same purple color as the towels hanging on the bar affixed to the freshly painted wall. How easily everything was erased. As if it never belonged to them. I thought, *old enemies and new friends have been their softest selves in this room*, how alive our vulnerability is, fragile as egg skin and just as transparent. I checked behind the shower curtain to make sure the tub was empty before I peed. I flushed and washed my hands, dried them on her towel. It was getting late and we needed to make dinner for our son, who was home playing Minecraft. I could see the blue light of our television from Leni's patio door. Back in the living room, we congratulated her on her new home, thanked her for inviting us, promised we'd do it again soon. Before I closed her front door I said, *I'm so glad you are here.*

Afterword

THAT FIRST SUMMER AFTER JIM'S DEATH, A BIRD FLEW into our yard and landed on my shoulder. It was a parakeet, small and blue and most certainly someone's pet who had escaped or been set free to fend for himself. He landed on my shoulder and did not move, so neither did I, awestruck at what felt miraculous.

I didn't know at first what to do. He didn't belong in our yard. Neither did he belong in a cage. But there he was, on my shoulder, impossible.

My husband and son went into the basement and found a small box. My in-laws, who were over for dinner, watched as I cupped the blue body in my right hand, his little bird heart a river against my fingers. I put him inside the box and loosely closed the lid.

Then I left to find him a home, something safer than a box or the backyard, until we could find the people who lost him. Did I mention it was the Fourth of July? The only store open did not have a birdcage, only a hamster habitat, but that seemed better than nothing.

On my way home, I wondered whether the bird was let free or if he had escaped. Maybe I was doing the absolute wrong thing, putting him in an enclosure. But if I went home, opened the box, and let him go, he would certainly die—a pet parakeet is not prepared for Connecticut weather, or hawks, or osprey, or feral cats.

I put posts on Facebook and Instagram. I called the exotic bird and fish store, the chain pet store, and several veterinarians' offices. No one seemed eager to help me. After two weeks, when still no one claimed them, I gave the bird to my mother.

From the bird's new home in an actual birdcage on my mother's kitchen counter, he sang to her. She was recently divorced from her second husband and living alone in a small tidy house with red shutters. She worried the bird might (also) be lonely, and so got another one from one of the pet stores I had called weeks before. The new parakeet was yellow and green. Their first night together, the little blue bird—brace yourselves—killed his new roommate. My mother woke to a streak of blood on their mirror, the new bird's yellow head submerged in the water bowl.

Two years later, my mother got married again, to a musician. She and the blue bird moved across town. For the rest of the bird's life, he spent the glow of sunny mornings on her husband's shoulder, looking outside through the windows of their screened-in porch.

Full bestiary, collected and alphabetized

 Ape: v. To imitate, to mimic (pretentiously, irrationally, or absurdly). To mimic the reality. (See also *parrot*.)

 Badger: v. To haggle, drive a bargain. Also, to pester, to bother, to ply with repeated and irritating requests to do something. Probably an allusion to the baiting of badgers by humans. (See also *fish*, also *clam*.) Uses of *badger* in the seventeenth century allude to the supposed tenacity of the animal's bite, gripping so hard its teeth meet.

 Bat: v. To hit away, to strike or hit a ball with a bat. There is also the US expression *to bat the eyes*, which is a fluttering of eyelashes seen as a way of flirting. *To bat*, then, can be an act of violence or an act of sex.

 Bear: v. To carry. From the Gothic *bairam*, in all senses, "to carry, to bring, endure, to give birth."

We bear the weight of; we bear the brunt of. The past tense of bear is *bore*, which possibly emerged from the middle English *borne* or *boren*. It is believed by some that *borne* meant carrying weight and *born* meant giving birth. Pregnancy is a weight borne before the baby is born. We bear children. We also bear arms.

Chicken (out): v. To withdraw from an activity.

Clam: v. Though obsolete now, to clam once meant to smear, daub, or spread unctuous matter on or with. Throughout its history, the verb form of clam is linked with its animal form: slimy and sticky, moist and gelatinous.

To bedaub a thing so that it sticks is to clam that thing together.

To clam up is to clamp a mouth shut, to be silent. It has also meant to clutch, grasp, or grope, because a clam is like a barnacle. Then, of course, it has always meant the act of catching the animals themselves. As in, *They went clamming at the beach*. A linguistic move as grotesque as it is efficient. (See also *fish*, also *badger*.)

Cock: v. To fight, wrangle, do battle. To behave boastfully, to swagger and strut, to brag, or crow over. (See also *crow*, also *swan*.)

This is an old word. Old as sunrises. In the fourteenth century, hay was cocked into conical heaps.

The use of cock as a synonym for *swagger* first appears in the sixteenth century. By the seventeenth century, it was used as coarse slang: to cock was to have sex.

In addition, to cock means to cause (especially a part of the body) to stick up in an assertive or jaunty way. To cock your head. This usage first appeared in the seventeenth century, so we've been cocking our heads and our hats for almost 400 years. We've been cocking guns since 1598. (To *cock about*, also called *dick about*, means to annoy a person or waste a person's time. See also *badger*.)

 Cow: v. "To depress with fear" (Johnson); to dispirit, overawe, intimidate.

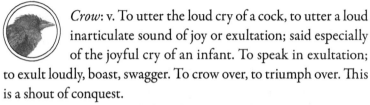 *Crow*: v. To utter the loud cry of a cock, to utter a loud inarticulate sound of joy or exultation; said especially of the joyful cry of an infant. To speak in exultation; to exult loudly, boast, swagger. To crow over, to triumph over. This is a shout of conquest.

Crows gather around their dead, an act that looks like mourning. Perhaps it is, though scientists believe they are actually trying to assess what happened in order to avoid the same fate. Crows do not want to die.

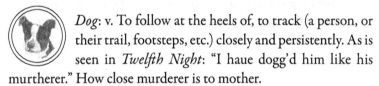 *Dog*: v. To follow at the heels of, to track (a person, or their trail, footsteps, etc.) closely and persistently. As is seen in *Twelfth Night*: "I haue dogg'd him like his murtherer." How close murderer is to mother.

There is an obsolete usage, from the early 1600s, where *to dog* meant *to haunt*. An invisible threat. More recently, it is used to mean to shirk, or to avoid. But *to dog* can also imply one is being a persistent source of distress to someone.

We also say, "to hound."

 Duck: v. To avoid getting hit.
Often yelled as a warning.
(See also *chicken*.)

 Ferret: v. First used to mean to hunt with ferrets. By the seventeenth century *to ferret* also meant to worry after. Or to drive away. A few decades earlier we see it used the way we do now, meaning to rummage or tease something out, but also to be restless with worry. It also appears that once, in 1699, ferreted meant cheated.

Ferrets were domesticated 2,500 years ago and used to hunt rabbits.

A coat made of ferret fur is called *fitch*, which seems like a way to make its skinning anonymous. A coat made of rabbit is still called rabbit. They have never been used to hunt anything.

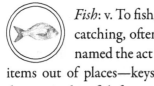 *Fish*: v. To fish, as a verb, sometimes refers to the act of catching, often with a hook, the noun version. We've named the act of killing fish after the casualty. We fish items out of places—keys from pockets, lost jewelry from sink drains. And we fish for compliments. This usage—fishing as eliciting a response or opinion—can be dated to 1570. In 1986, my uncle swallowed a goldfish whole, right in front of me, and expected me to clap. I called him a monster, wished the fish could swim up and out of his body.

 Fly: v. To travel through the air. This word is as old as Beowulf, both as a verb and as a name for a winged insect.

Dreaming about flying is common, and analysts link these dreams to thoughts of freedom. Everyone wants to fly, though no one wants to be a fly.

 Gander: v. Older than the verb *to swan*, though the meaning is the same: to wander aimlessly, in body or in speech. But also to look at, as in "take a gander." Looking can be violent, as in staring. The "taking" of a look also implies a lack of consent. A gander is a male goose. (See also *goose*.)

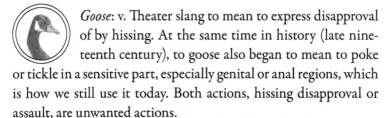

Goose: v. Theater slang to mean to express disapproval of by hissing. At the same time in history (late nineteenth century), to goose also began to mean to poke or tickle in a sensitive part, especially genital or anal regions, which is how we still use it today. Both actions, hissing disapproval or assault, are unwanted actions.

There used to be several geese wandering the green space in my town, Mother Goose Geese we called them. They did not hiss, though they waddled slowly across streets, blocking traffic. The mayor paid someone to oil their eggs and now we have no geese.

Hawk: v. To pursue or attack while flying.
To sell in the street by yelling about one's wares.

Hog: *v.* To keep something selfishly to oneself. Before hogging was a selfish act, it meant "to clean a ship's bottom or sides with a special broom, also called a hog." In fact, the use of hog as a verb often has to do with ships. Pigs are very good swimmers. *To hog* has meant to cause a ship to arch upwards in the middle and droop at the ends as a result of fracture from excess weight. It has also meant to arch the back, to cut a horse's mane close to the neck, and to keep a lamb over winter for sale the following year. *To hog* is used in the sport of curling when one plays the stone with too little force to clear the hog line. We currently use it to mean "to use extensively," as in *to hog* resources. Using *to hog* to mean to greedily or selfishly appropriate, monopolize, or use the road in a reckless and inconsiderate manner is originally an American term.

Lark: v. To play tricks, frolic. To ride in a frolicsome manner; to ride across country (as in "lark about").

To ride (a horse) across the country. This makes sense when we also consider that *to lark* has also meant to clear a fence with a flying leap.

To lark a fence, one becomes like a horse breaking free from confinement.

Lastly, to make fun of, to tease a person sportively. I think teasing is cruel, as a sport or otherwise.

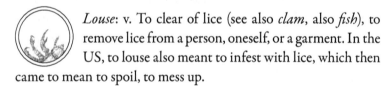

Leech: v. At one time *to leech* meant to heal, to cure, because we used leeches to drain the bad out of blood; we used them on our bodies because we believed they could help us remove the toxins that ailed us. *To leech* someone was to care about their well-being. We stopped believing in the leech as a tool for healing in the late nineteenth century and now we only use *to leech* when we mean to latch on, like a parasite. To be parasitic.

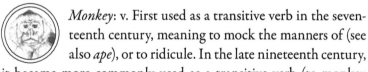

Louse: v. To clear of lice (see also *clam*, also *fish*), to remove lice from a person, oneself, or a garment. In the US, to louse also meant to infest with lice, which then came to mean to spoil, to mess up.

Monkey: v. First used as a transitive verb in the seventeenth century, meaning to mock the manners of (see also *ape*), or to ridicule. In the late nineteenth century, it became more commonly used as a transitive verb (to monkey around), which means to fool around, or even to horse around.

Parrot: v. To chatter, to talk incessantly, inconsequentially, to gossip. The *OED* lists this 1701 sentence from T. Baker's *Humour of Age* (1701) as an example: "The

Play-house! Ay, that's the Place where such young bold Slutts as you are nurs'd up in your Impudence; where you parrot to the Men."

To parrot insinuates a mocking, a lack of substance. There once was a parrot called Alex, who learned not only to talk in a language his handler could understand, but to communicate abstractly. There are videos of Alex on YouTube, and I am drawn to the one where he chooses between various objects: not just a green thing, or a block, but the green block. His feathers are ragged. After every question his handler asks him, Alex responds, *I wanna go back. Go back.* And maybe he meant his cage, but maybe not. He died when he was only thirty-one. (See also *ape*.)

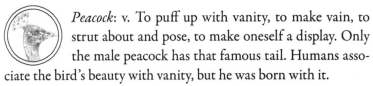 *Peacock*: v. To puff up with vanity, to make vain, to strut about and pose, to make oneself a display. Only the male peacock has that famous tail. Humans associate the bird's beauty with vanity, but he was born with it.

In Australia, *to peacock* means to obtain the best portions of a tract of land, especially to make the remainder of the surrounding land of lower value to other people. There are so many different types of vanity.

Pig: v. Obsolete now, but *to pig* has history as a derogatory expression of a woman giving birth, as is seen in this scrap of a letter, from 1843: "Tom told me this morning that his wife had been very ill during the night. I said, 'Has she pigged?'"

Pig has also meant to huddle, to live, or to sleep together, especially in crowded or dirty conditions. Frequently with *together*; occasionally with *in*. Also, though rare, with *along*. *To pig along* is to live in a simple, unsophisticated, or slovenly fashion. We have forgotten, or rather, we refuse to remember, that pigs are smart, emotive, compassionate. Clean, too.

A contemporary usage combines *to pig* with *out*, as in "to pig out," as in to gorge, to eat something quickly. (See also *wolf*.)

 Pigeon: v. Rare, obsolete really. *To pigeon* once meant, colloquially, to intentionally cheat, to swindle, especially at cards. (See also *ferret*.) Journalists used to use it as a verb meaning to smuggle a report. Pigeon keeping was once popular in New York City, though it has gotten too expensive to do so. Now they fly above those rooftops, look down on a city in lockdown.

 Ram: v. To batter. To ram as in to beat down the earth and ram as in a male sheep both appeared in writing around the same time. Now *to ram*, also *to ram in*, evokes a smashing. Ram it in there, ram it with your car. Rams will smash into each other, a fight for dominance.

Also: to force (a bullet, bolt, charge, etc.) into a firearm, usually by means of a ramrod.

 Seal: v. To close (with a seal). If an agreement is sealed with a handshake, that agreement is considered binding. You can press a seal to close something up; to seal wood, use varnish. *To seal* is to smother.

In elementary school in the late '80s/early '90s, we swapped valentines stamped with the wet-sounding acronym SWAK, which meant sealed with a kiss.

 Slug: *v*. To punch. But also, and perhaps more closely aligned to the animal itself, to move idly, lazily, slowly. Or, to be lazy or slow. Or, to hinder or delay.

To load a gun with slugs is called slugging, though a bullet moves at about 1,700 miles per hour.

To slug it out means to fight it out.

To drug or exploit, like by slipping something into someone's drink in a bar, is called slugging. Additionally, to drink quickly, especially beer, is known as slugging.

A slug is like a snail without a shell. It is completely vulnerable to the world.

 Snake: v. To twist, to wind. To move in a manner suggestive of a snake.

An old American slang term: to beat, thrash.

Perseus beheaded Medusa in a death so violent it forced the births of her children through the wound of her neck. Perseus stuffed her head into a sack and first used her to turn his enemies to stone, then to rescue Andromeda, and finally as a gift to Athena.

Another Americanism: to take out surreptitiously. To steal or pilfer.

Intransitive: to skulk or sneak. (I am noticing right now that sneak is an anagram of snake.)

 Squirrel: v. To go around in circles. To save or hoard.

A list of things I have squirreled away includes: seashells, notes from my husband, bad dreams, old photographs, my son's baby teeth, vintage postcards.

Squirrel fur was coveted in medieval Europe, and was, perhaps, how leprosy was transferred from animal to human. A postmortem revenge.

Swallow: v. To bring into the stomach through the throat or gullet. The opposite of to spit.

Figuratively, *to swallow* is used as a verb to describe ways things disappear. (See also *squirrel*.) To swallow one's spittle is to suppress one's anger, to swallow the anchor is to quit sailing. A swallow is a bird so aerodynamic it hunts on the wing. (See also *hawk*.) So many versions of consuming.

Wolf: v. To devour ravenously. (See also *pig*.)

In one version of the story of the three little pigs, a wolf destroys the first two pigs' homes and eats them, a punishment for their laziness. But the reason the pigs were on their own to begin with is because their mother didn't have enough food to feed them. Really, then, they are products of a failed system. In some other versions of this story, the lazy pigs aren't eaten but escape to the house where their responsible brother lives, and the three cook up the wolf and eat him for dinner.

 Worm: v. To hunt or to catch worms. (See also *fish*, also *clam*, also *louse*.) Yet, *to worm* also means to be devoured by worms. Another verb of contradiction.

Also, *to worm* is to pry secrets from a person. This is an extraction, a removal of what should remain within. (See also *badger*.)

But *to worm* is not only to pry loose another's secrets. One can worm anything out, though sometimes we say someone will worm their way in. Both require the use of pressure, the use of force. Money, labor, land. Time, too, is wormed away. Language itself is an extraction wormed from culture and reimagined. (See also *ape*.) To worm is to manipulate. (See also *snake*, also *fish*.)

Acknowledgments

LIKE ALL PROJECTS, THIS ONE STARTED OUT AS AN IDEA, one that seemed important, but abstract. I am eternally grateful to all at Wilfrid Laurier University Press for seeing the possibility within and helping me shape it into existence. Thank you especially to Siobhan McMenemy, Anne Brackenbury, Sonja Boon, and Clare Hitchens.

Thank you to my colleagues in the Department of Languages and Literature at Sacred Heart University, especially Peter Sinclair and Mark Beekey, who supported this project from the very beginning. Thank you to the folks at Fordham where some of this writing began, especially Lenny Cassuto, Moshe Gold, and Elizabeth Stone.

And to the Fall 2023 section of English 271—Ayasha, Grace, Julia P., Tori, and Julia Y., thank you for your ideas and creativity and for trusting me with your work. You all are brilliant.

To Eugenia Kim, who, during a phone call years ago, listened to me talk in circles about this idea and stopped me mid-sentence to say, "do this now."

To all the friends who've helped me along the way, especially Michael, Adrian, Cory, Kelly, Terri, Charlie, Beth, Emily, and Megs. I am so grateful for you all.

And to my family. The years I've written about here may have felt like a nightmare, but you two are a dream from which I hope I never wake up. I love you both fiercely. Thank you for this life.

Notes

I.   What happened (to badger/to ape)

In my search to understand what happened those three years we lived beside Jim and Wes, I read and reread books and articles, certain I'd find myself closer to an explanation if I just kept reading. But as I collected pages of notes, I found myself moving toward an idea only to double back and pause, rewind, repeat myself, and then change course, endlessly evaluating my own ideas against those of others. One of the hardest parts about writing through these memories was noticing how my own repetitions, my own tendency to fixate or obsess on a detail, reminded me of the men I was writing about. The other difficulty was reinhabiting the way my body felt back then—endlessly on edge, constantly waiting for disaster. (Although, sometimes motherhood, and other times being an American, also feels like this.) Once, midway through writing the second draft of this book, I went to my son's swim meet with my mother. I couldn't take my eyes off the pool, worrying he would hit his head, wondering if he'd been under the water for too long. My mother, though, kept looking behind us, not at the pool, but the door. Irritated, I asked her if she was waiting for someone. *No*, she said, *I just like to know where the exits are in case someone shows up with a gun.*

These pages vacillate through time, revisiting old ideas with new insights, tangling and untangling what happened, not just in my neighborhood, but throughout history. The books and essays mentioned in this chapter, especially Pumla Dineo Gqola's *Female Fear Factory: Unraveling Patriarchy's Cultures of Violence*, Rosemarie Garland-Thomson's *Staring: How We Look*, bell hooks's "Eating the Other: Desire and Resistance," and Virginie Despentes's essay collection *King Kong Theory*, will continue to be referenced, each time opening a new door, but never closing the old one.

NOTES TO I. WHAT HAPPENED

1   Gqola, *Female Fear Factory*, xviii.

2   Garland-Thomson, *Staring*, 39.

3   Gqola, *Female Fear Factory*, 67.

4   Despentes, *King Kong Theory*, 28.

5   hooks, "Eating the Other," 368.

6   Donald Trump (@realDonalTrump), Twitter (now X), December 12, 2019, 7:22 a.m., https://x.com/realDonaldTrump/status/1205100602025545730?lang=en.

7   Senator Mitch McConnell is married to an Asian American woman.

8   Khaleda Rahman. "Close-Up Video Shows Texas Floating Barrier Has Circular Saws." *Newsweek*, August 9, 2023.

9   Grammarians call the verbing of a noun denominalization.

10   *PBS NewsHour*, "American Black women," June 28, 2023.

11   In late summer, 2024, fourteen US states have total abortion bans. These states are: Alabama, Arkansas, Idaho, Indiana, Kentucky, Louisiana, Mississippi, Missouri, North

Dakota, Oklahoma, South Dakota, Tennessee, Texas, and West Virginia.

12   Burton and Mawani, *Animalia*, 4–5.

13   I looked up what this shade of yellow is called in *The Secret Lives of Color* and found the shade that most clearly matches is called "Imperial Yellow."

14   Burton and Mawani, *Animalia*.

15   Carol J. Adams, *The Sexual Politics of Meat*, 22.

16   Gumbs, *Undrowned*, 31.

17   In fact, by the 1780s, up to 90 percent of families in Lyon and Paris sent their children to wet nurses. This included not just aristocrats, but farmers, clergy, and artisans. (Schiebinger, *Nature's Body: Gender in the Making of Modern Science*.)

18   Clare, *Brilliant Imperfection*, 6.

19   Though the US has a Family Medical Leave Act, it only requires employers to hold an employee's job for twelve weeks post birth or adoption. It does not require those employers to pay those parents while they are away.

20   Anderson, "The Last Two Northern White Rhinos on Earth," *New York Times Magazine*, 2021.

II.   On boundaries (to bear/to pig)

This chapter is the first of several about boundaries. A broken boundary can be a rupture, but it can also be a release; an established boundary can protect, though it can also trap. When speaking of boundaries we are speaking of bodies—of land or animal or human animal.

Both Eli Clare in *Brilliant Imperfection: Grappling with Cure* and Eula Biss in *On Immunity: An Inoculation* helped me think about bodies. From Clare, a deeper understanding of the ableism inherent in everything from health care to advertising, and how that thinking shapes the way bodies are treated. From Biss, a history of inoculations, which is to say, like Clare, a grappling with the relationship between care and harm. I would also recommend Anne Boyer's *The Undying* (Farrar, Straus and Giroux, 2019) and Leah Lakshmi Piepzna-Samarasinha's *Care Work: Dreaming Disability Justice* (Arsenal Pulp Press, 2018) for more work on harm and healing.

In different ways, Clare and Biss not only write about health care, but also skin. Clare considers how skin bleaching creams are marketed as a "cure," a way to lighten skin in a culture that deems dark skin a problem. Biss writes about the skin, vaccines, and diseases, research she began because she was curious about the vaccines available for her newborn son. She calls birth an inoculation, the baby leaving a sterile womb to be exposed, in the birth process, to microbes that will enter through their skin and protect them for years.

However, in a society built on white supremacy, whiteness is normalized and creates a culture where nonwhite people are seen as inferior. Skin is a barrier to safety or a gateway to privilege. Skin is a boundary, the human animal's largest organ, its job to provide a protective barrier from the physical world, but the skin is vulnerable and easily broken. To write about harm, which is where this story starts, I need to also write about care, even if I am not sure that's where it ends.

NOTES TO II. ON BOUNDARIES

1   Clare, *Brilliant Imperfection*, 30.

2   Duffy, "Blue Bloods," *Johns Hopkins Magazine,* 2021.

3   Clare, *Brilliant Imperfection*, 31.

4   Eisner, "Coastal biomedical labs," *NPR*, June 2023.

5   Clare, *Brilliant Imperfection*, 23.

6   We recently watched the Ari Aster folk-horror film *Midsommar*, where one of the Americans is stitched inside

a disemboweled bear before he is burnt to death inside a house. Trapped inside twice.

7   Arendt, "The Concept of History," 572.

8   *About Milford*, https://www.ci.milford.ct.us/home/pages/about-milford.

9   Arvin et al., "Decolonizing Feminism," 12.

10   Arvin et al., "Decolonizing Feminism," 12.

11   Pierce, "Revolutionary War prisoners," July 4, 2017.

12   Biss, *On Immunity*.

13   There are two vials of smallpox in labs, one in the US and one in Russia. Whether we should keep them for possible future research and vaccine development or destroy them to eliminate any possible accidents is hotly contested.

14   Clare, *Brilliant Imperfection*, 23.

15   Taylor Swift ft. Bon Iver, "Exile," *Folklore* 2020.

III.   *On gossip (to parrot/to slug/to swallow)*

"We use the term civilized often as a synonym for well-mannered, wild as another word for uncouth." I wrote this sentence in response to Jack Halberstam's work on the wild/civilized opposition. As noted, the very idea of wilderness/wildness is a white settler colonizer concept, an idea that is rooted in the idea of conquest and expansion. Or, as William Cronon said, "wilderness is quite profoundly a human creation—indeed, the creation of very particular human cultures at very particular moments in human history."

In settler colonizer literature and language, wilderness is in turns romanticized, feared, and destroyed. In Indigenous teachings and practices, there is no wilderness, but rather community and kinship. In addition to the work already cited in these pages, I recommend reading the following books, all by Indigenous women whose work has been integral to my own continued unlearning of the concept of wilderness and white supremacist settler colonizer thinking: Leanne Betasamosake Simpson in *As We Have Always Done* writes, "Meaning...is derived not through content or data or even theory in a Western context, which by nature is decontextualized knowledge, but through a compassionate web of interdependent relationships that are different and valuable because of difference"; Stephanie Rutherford's *Villain, Vermin, Icon, Kin*, whose work on wolves shows how settler approaches to dealing with so-called "wildness out of place" led to wildlife annihilation, all of which is part and parcel to a colonizer narrative of conquest; and Patty Krawec in *Becoming Kin* writes in her opening chapter, "The world is alive with beings that are other than human, and we are all related, with responsibilities to each other."

NOTES TO III. ON GOSSIP

1   Louise Collins, "Gossip: A Feminist Defense," 106–14.

2   Halberstam, *Wild Things*, ix.

3   For suggested readings on this topic, please see notes above.

4   Prince, "Renaissance Invention," 2017.

5   New Art Publications, "BOMB Magazine," March 4, 2024.

6   Clark, "'Their Negro Nanny,'" 541.

7   According to the Pew Research Center, 47 percent of White women voted for Donald Trump in the 2016 election. In 2020, that number jumped to 53 percent. (Pew Research Center, "An examination of the 2016 electorate, based on validated voters," September 2018, and "Behind Biden's 2020 Victory: An examination of the 2020 electorate, based on validated voters," June 2021.)

8   Clark, "'Their Negro Nanny,'" 546.

9   Please read Clark's full study on the role of gossip in Nanny's case: "'Their Negro Nanny'."

10   Tatar, *The Heroine with 1,001 Faces*, 121.

11   Tatar, *The Heroine with 1,001 Faces*, 123.

12   The T.J. Elliott translation of the thirteenth century's *A Medieval Bestiary* includes allegories, which might also be thought of as little gossip-stories.

IV. On performance (to cow/to cock/to clam)

In the second chapter, I backed into a mention of cannibalism after writing about the implied relationship between Jim and his mother. I am thinking about the links between consummation and consumption, sex and food, morality and taboo, motherhood and survival. I think it's intimacy I'm interested in. What happens when closeness goes too far? What are human animals capable of, for pleasure or survival? These questions are other ways to think about boundaries. This chapter is partially about performance art, which often asks similar questions. For further reading, I recommend Lauren Elkin's *Art Monsters: Unruly Bodies in Feminist Art* as well as Irina Aristarkhova's essay "Eating the Mother" from the collection *Meat! A Transnational Analysis*. Aristarkhova opens her essay with a description of Jess Dobkin's performance piece *The Lactation Station Breast Milk Bar* (2006–2016), a collaborative work wherein an artist offered (consensually donated) breast milk to the audience as if it were a wine tasting. Aristarkhova uses this performance piece to explore questions of cannibalism and breast-feeding, asking "Is the mother food? And if the mother is food, then what kind of food: meat, drink, solid, liquid?"

NOTES ON IV. ON PERFORMANCE

1   Ward, *No Innocent Bystanders*, 124.

2   Much can be found online about Truth's speech, as it is in the public domain. The online magazine *Learning for Justice* has

transcripts and teaching resources. https://learningforjustice
.org/classroom-resources/texts/aint-i-a-woman.

3   It wasn't. I had remembered this train incident as happening
     after we'd moved in. I had remembered it within a time
     context that let me already understand the brothers as
     invasive and capable of harm. Thinking now, knowing that
     this was, in fact, our first encounter with their antics, with
     their intent to intimidate us out of our house by making
     us uncomfortable, by making us aware of their capabilities
     to breach what we thought was private, changes my
     understanding of the memory, but I can't divorce myself from
     interpreting the tone, from separating hindsight and insight.

4   Cha, "Mouth to Mouth" via mplus.org.

5   Claycomb, *Lives in Play*, 67.

6   Hong, *Minor Feelings*, 156.

7   Hong, *Minor Feelings*, 165.

8   In this same essay, Hong also writes that Sanza's conviction
     was overturned, in part because he was "polite" to the other
     women he raped, which stood in opposition to the brutal
     way he raped Cha. How can someone rape politely?

9   Biss, "Time and Distance Overcome," 2.

10   Biss, "Time and Distance Overcome," 2.

11   "Self-Portrait," by Emma Sulkowicz. Performed at Coagula
     Curatorial in Los Angeles, February 27–April 3, 2016.

12   Ward, *No Innocent Bystanders*, 114.

V.   On catching and being caught (to dog/to bat/to fly/to peacock/to gander/to squirrel)

In a very early attempt at writing this book, I paralleled our
experiences with the neighbors with an analysis of Mary Shelley's
Frankenstein. Those thoughts don't fit in this book, though if I could

have found a way, I would have included them in this glutinous, monstrous chapter. Even without explicit mention, much of Shelley's book lives in these pages—thoughts about the environment, exile, the enslaved, wealth, empathy, mother figures, the responsibility of science, morality and ethics, ableism, rage, beauty. Crossed boundaries, power, care. For further reading on how works like Shelley's help us understand our own worlds, I recommend Jennifer Clements's essay, "How Science Fiction Helps Us Reimagine Our Moral Relations with Animals" from the 2015 *Journal of Animal Ethics*.

One last thing. This chapter is primarily about looking—dead bugs under glass, the surveillance camera. Looking, though, is different than being seen. When the monster in *Frankenstein* enters the hut where the blind old man lives with his children, he feels companionship for the first time. But when Felix and Agatha return, they look at him and scream. The monster runs away, shunned, and vows "everlasting war against the species." This is not a promise born from rejection, but shame, of being looked at, but not seen.

NOTES ON V. ON CATCHING AND BEING CAUGHT

1   Despentes, "You Can't Rape a Woman's Who's a Total Slut," *King Kong Theory*, 32.

2   *The Washington Post* tracks fatal police shootings in the US. Since 2015, 10,080 people have been killed. Although half of the people the police have killed are White, Black Americans, who make up about 14 percent of the population, are killed at more than twice the rate of White Americans. Hispanic Americans are also killed by police at disproportionate rates. Information regularly updated at https://www.washingtonpost.com/graphics/investigations/police-shootings-database/.

3   Darwin, *The Expression of the Emotions in Man and Animals*.

4   Schiebinger, *Nature's Body*, 1993.
5   Derrida, *The Animal That Therefore I Am*, 11.
6   It seems important to note that the cat's name was Logos.
7   The third of the soul he called the "sensitive soul."
8   Schiebinger, *Nature's Body*, 81.
9   Simpson, *As We Have Always Done*, 154.
10   From Masson and McCarthy's *When Elephants Weep*,
       which argues for the study of animal emotions and
       was published in 1995, the year after my own elephant
       anthropomorphizing.
11   Derrida, *The Animal*, 28.

VI.   On fear (to hawk)

My younger brother once told me he thinks women should "just
carry guns to protect themselves." However, studies show guns
almost never stop sexual assault, and when women own firearms, it
is more likely their guns will be used against them.

My father left us when my brother was ten, and from then on, he
was the only boy in a house full of women. Around the time my father
left, we all watched the movie *Edward Scissorhands* (1990) together.
He was terrified, but I (age sixteen) thought it was romantic, which
is to say, my brother and I have conflicting capacities for fear and
violence. For more reading on horror movies, growing up, and girl-
hood, read Gina Nutt's *Night Rooms*. For more reading about horror
movies and suburban families, read Pat Gill's "The Monstrous Years:
Teens, Slasher Films, and the Family." For more reading on suburbs,
in addition to Leslie Kern's *Feminist City*, read Alex Krieger's "'Grace
Dwelling in It': The Romance of the Suburb" from *City on a Hill:
Urban Idealism in America from the Puritans to the Present*, and Jan
Nijman and Tom Clery's "The United States: Suburban Imaginaries
and Metropolitan Realities" in *Suburban Governance: A Global View*.

NOTES TO VI. ON FEAR

1   For statistics on sexual violence, visit the National Sexual Assault Hotline, https://www.rainn.org/statistics/victims-sexual-violence. For help, visit the chat feature on this website or call 800-656-HOPE (4673).

2   Gqola, *Female Fear Factory*, 77.

3   According to 2016 FBI data, White men were responsible for over 67 percent of US rapes, 62.8 percent of aggravated assault cases, and 59 percent of the country's violent crimes. In 1997, when I took this class, White men were responsible for 58.2 percent of rapes, 61.2 percent of aggravated assaults, and 56.8 percent of violent crimes.

4   Despentes, *King Kong Theory*, 40.

5   Despentes, *King Kong Theory*, 41.

6   Gqola, *Female Fear Factory*, 18.

7   The knife entering might be read as a rape, too; a punishment for her sexuality.

8   When she told me this, I wondered if they might actually have the ability to listen to our phone calls.

9   Garland-Thomson, *Staring*, 33.

10   Garland-Thomson, *Staring*, 41.

11   Garland-Thomson, *Staring*, 41.

12   This fear was made larger when police falsely claimed Jack the Ripper's victims to be prostitutes.

13   This did not happen elsewhere in Europe. Most other European countries saw the rise in industry and what rippled outward—theatre, art, etc.—as progress.

14   In the United States, massive SUVs are frequently driven by families; one of the largest is the Chevy Suburban.

15   Thrasher, *Black Suburbia*, June 2016. Schomburg Center for Research in Black Culture, New York Public Library.

16   Those small Cape Cod and ranch houses are hard to come by and are no longer popular in new construction, one of the many reasons homeownership is not possible for many Americans.

17   TallBear, "Disrupting Settlement, Sex, and Nature," 17:04. https://indigenousfutures.net/wp-content/uploads/2016/10/Kim_TallBear.pdf.

18   Gqola, *Female Fear Factory*, 16.

19   As I write this, in the late summer of 2024, a French woman in her seventies named Gisèle Pelicot is testifying at the trial of her husband, Dominique Pelicot, who slipped drugs into her wine for years so that she could be raped by the men he sold her to. In addition to her husband, fifty men are standing trial.

VII. On boundaries, again (to seal/to lark/to wolf)

Sarah Rose Etter's novel *The Book of X* is not only a consideration of meat, capitalism, and the scrutiny of women's bodies, it is also a book about chronic pain. Every month, I lose a string of days to migraine. Each one follows the same pattern: First an aura of wavy lines disrupts my vision, then numbness travels down the left side of my face and through my arm. My speech patterns are disrupted, words come out backwards or slurred or missing. Lastly, a sharp headache settles between my eyes and jaw and brings with it a feeling of sadness that stays for hours. Deadlines, projects, mothering, grading, being a partner, class prep, writing, and art making—all parts of my life—must be put on hold for four hours a day, five or six days in a row, every three to four weeks. Every three months, I see a neurologist to adjust my medication. He says this is manageable. A few favorite books about women's health include Sonya Huber's *Pain Woman Takes Your Keys* (University of Nebraska Press, 2017), Porochista Khakpour's *Sick* (Harper Perennial, 2018), Esmé Weijun Wang's *The Collected Schizophrenias* (Graywolf Press, 2019), Anne Elizabeth Moore's *Body Horror*, and Lisa Olstein's *Pain Studies* (Bellevue Literary Press, 2020).

NOTES ON VII. ON BOUNDARIES, AGAIN

1   Using the term "gaslighting" to mean emotional manipulation comes from a 1930s British play by the same name about a husband who manipulates his wife into thinking she is losing her mind (per the Illinois Coalition Against Domestic Violence).
2   Lara, "Habermas's Concept of the Public Sphere and the New Feminist Agenda," August 11, 2019.
3   It isn't unusual for victims of assault to be blamed for what happened to them. People will ask, *Why didn't you scream/ fight back/run away*? But anyone who has feared for their life will tell you that not moving is often the only way to survive.
4   Carol J. Adams, *The Sexual Politics of Meat*, 64.
5   hooks, *Ain't I a Woman*, 112.
6   Sinclair, *The Jungle*, 37.
7   Scott Derrick, "Gender in the Jungle," in *The Jungle* (W.W. Norton, 2003), 500.
8   Etter, *The Book of X*, 5.
9   Kimmerer, *Braiding Sweetgrass*, 177.
10   Kimmerer, *Braiding Sweetgrass*, 190.

VIII. On boundaries, once more (to fish/to ram/to chicken (out)/to duck)

I live near New Haven, and we go to the Yale Art Gallery whenever we can. There are two Magrittes in their collection: *La boîte de Pandore* (Pandora's box) and *Le Principe d'Archimède* (Archimedes' principle). The latter is my favorite of the two. In it, apples are suspended over a shallow bowl with a high pedestal. The light is dramatic, but I am drawn to the painting's darkness. The suspended apples have leaves, like wings, but the apples in the bowl have no leaves, and only a hint of where there once was stem.

In the foreword of the Museum of Modern Art's book *Magritte: The Mystery of the Ordinary, 1926-1938*, the editors describe the exhibition of his work as "investigating the strategies Magritte used to *defamiliarize* the familiar, including displacement, doubling, isolation, metamorphosis, 'misnaming' objects, and representing visions seen in half-waking states." This list is what I want this book to do, too.

For more reading on surrealism, please read Whitney Chadwick's extensive and canonical *Women Artists and the Surrealist Movement*. For more reading on Magritte, please read the biography *Magritte: A Life* by Alex Danchev and *René Magritte: Selected Writings*, especially his very strong and often funny thoughts on architecture and decor.

NOTES ON VIII. ON BOUNDARIES, ONCE MORE

1   Inside our house, my own child, now fifteen, has just passed my same height.
2   Danchev, *Magritte: A Life*, 20.
3   Danchev, *Magritte: A Life*, 20.
4   The trunk became so rotted we had to cut it down before it collapsed. The stump has since decayed into the ground; there is no longer any evidence of its existence.

5   Spiegel, *The Dreaded Comparison*, 33.
6   Spiegel, *The Dreaded Comparison*, 98.
7   Nelson, *The Art of Cruelty*, 175.
8   According to the Sanctuary for Families, of all femicide cases in high-income countries, 70 percent occur in the US. https://sanctuaryforfamilies.org/femicide-epidemic.
9   Michael Adams, *In Praise of Profanity*, 121.
10   The full quote is: "The riskiness of using what in other instances is lexically profane corresponds to the event causing our anger, anxiety, or frustration—extraordinary events call for extraordinary measures."
11   In order to avoid exposing anyone's identity, the citation for this article has been omitted.

IX.   *On paranoia and revenge (to crow)*

In the years it took me to write this, I kept saying to myself: Be gentle. In part, this was a way to keep myself from falling back into the sharp feeling of violence I was writing about. But also, as I revise and edit and update the atrocities on one page with a more recent, more violent atrocity, I need to remember that I must do whatever is in my power to make changes. I live a life of great privilege and gentleness is often within my reach. I must spread it to others. Poetry is the language of grace and reverence and truth, and shortly after Sinéad O'Connor died, Erika Meitner wrote an elegy to her (published in *Electric Literature*, August 9, 2023). In her poem, she too writes of grief, climate catastrophe, lanternflies, and violence. I give you this excerpt, a gift of gentle language, though please go read the rest of the poem: "& Sinéad, the invasive/species are every-where—the spotted/lanternflies too that I'm supposed to kill/on sight, but who has the heart/for that kind of violence. I wish/I had your conviction & righteousness."

NOTES ON IX. ON PARANOIA AND REVENGE

1   According to a local Baltimore news station, in 2024 these numbers are dwindling due to a naturally occurring fungus, increased populations of praying mantises, and a change in the diets of some birds.

2   Kimmerer, *Braiding Sweetgrass*, 183.

3   Sedgwick, *Touching Feeling*, 64.

4   Despentes, *King Kong Theory*, 40.

5   Jeanne McDermott, in *FACES* by Nancy Burson and used by Rosemarie Garland-Thomson as an epigraph in *Staring: How We Look*.

6   Geary, *I Is an Other*, 5.

7   Using animals as metaphors is a cross-cultural practice, though translating from one to another can be troublesome and problematic, as Mohamed Mansouri points out in "Animal Metaphor and Cultural Bias: Implications for the Translator."

8   Emphasis mine. From Poe, *The Tell-Tale Heart*, 5.

9   Emphasis mine. Sinclair, *The Jungle*, 153.

10   Sedgwick, *Touching Feeling*, 128.

11   Belcourt, *A History of My Brief Body*, 12.

12   de Beauvoir, *A Very Easy Death*, 106.

X.   *On continuation (to ferret/to leech)*

I will forever be fascinated by the bestiary, by all the ways human animals find to wonder about the world and then try to make sense of it. I love the way we combine language and art, the way we take old forms and make them new. Please read these bestiaries and bestiary-esque books: K-Ming Chang's *Bestiary: A Novel* (One World, 2020), Lily Hoang's *A Bestiary*, Elena Passarello's *Animals Strike*

Curious Poses, and Nuar Alsadir's *Animal Joy: A Book of Laughter* (Graywolf Press, 2022).

NOTES ON X. ON CONTINUATION

1 Vyse, *Superstition*, 14.

2 It was also considered heretical to deny the existence of witches.

3 Judson, "A Commencement Is Also a Memorial For 8th Year in a Row," *New York Times*, June 24, 1996.

4 Foucault, "The Simplest of Pleasures," https://www .generation-online.org/p/fp_foucault13.htm.

5 Probyn, *Blush: Faces of Shame*, 14.

6 Groff, "Flower Hunters," in *Florida*, 161.

7 Arvin et al., "Decolonizing Feminism: Challenging Connections between Settler Colonialism and Heteropatriarchy," 24.

8 Weber and Stengle, "Kate Cox sought an abortion in Texas," December 12, 2023.

9 According to their website, the Environmental Protection Agency refers to trash as MSW, which is an abbreviation for municipal solid waste. MSW is the blanket term for items consumers throw away after use, like bottles and boxes, food, grass clippings, sofas, computers, tires, and refrigerators. MSW does not include everything that might be landfilled at the local level, such as construction and demolition debris, municipal wastewater sludge, and other non-hazardous wastes.

10 I read recently in Daniel Heath Justice's book *Why Indigenous Literatures Matter* that apocalypse stories are places "where white people return to a fetishized frontier to carve a new, righteous patriarchy out of the ruin that was civilization."

Bibliography

About Milford, Milford, CT. n.d. Accessed February 2021. https://www
    .ci.milford.ct.us/home/pages/about-milford.

About the USPHS Syphilis Study, Tuskegee University. n.d. Accessed
    February 2023. https://tuskegee.edu/about-us/
    centers-of-excellence/bioethics-center/about-the-usphs
    -syphilis-study.

Abramović, Marina. *On Rhythm 0 (1974)*, via Vimeo. Accessed June 2022.
    https://vimeo.com/101920368.

Adams, Carol J. *The Sexual Politics of Meat: A Feminist-Vegetarian Critical
    Theory*. Continuum, 2000.

Adams, Michael. *In Praise of Profanity*. Oxford University Press, 2016.

Ahern, Maureen V., and Don L. F. Nilsen. "A Comparison of Animal
    Dead Metaphors in English and Spanish Speech." *Bilingual Review/
    La Revista Bilingüe* 3, no. 2 (1976): 163–75.

Anderson, Sam. "The Last Two Northern White Rhinos on Earth." *The
    New York Times*. January 6, 2021. Updated June 15, 2023.

Arendt, Hannah. "The Concept of History." In *Between Past and Future*.
    Penguin Classics, 2006.

Aristarkhova, Irina. "Eating the Mother." In *Meat!: A Transnational
    Analysis*. Duke University Press, 2021.

Arvin, Maile, Eve Tuck, and Angie Morrill. "Decolonizing Feminism: Challenging Connections between Settler Colonialism and Heteropatriarchy." *Feminist Formations* 25, no. 1 (2013): 8–34.

Barthes, Roland. *Roland Barthes by Roland Barthes*. Translated by Richard Howard. Farrar, Straus and Giroux, Inc., 1977.

Belcourt, Billy-Ray. *A History of My Brief Body*. Two-Dollar Radio, 2020.

Bennett, Geoff, host, *PBS NewsHour* podcast, "American Black women face high rates of maternal mortality." June 28, 2023.

Biss, Eula. *On Immunity: An Inoculation*. Graywolf Press, 2014.

Biss, Eula. "Time and Distance Overcome." In *Notes from No Man's Land: American Essays*. Graywolf Press, 2009.

Boon, Sonja. *What the Oceans Remember: Searching for Belonging and Home*. Wilfrid Laurier University Press, 2019.

Burton, Antoinette, and Renisa Mawani, eds. *Animalia: An Anti-Imperial Bestiary for Our Times*. Duke University Press, 2020.

Carson, Rachel. *Rachel Carson: The Sea Trilogy (LOA #352): Under the Sea-Wind/The Sea Around Us/The Edge of the Sea*. Library of America, 2021.

Cha, Theresa Hak Kyung. "Mouth to Mouth." Video. 1975. https://mplus .org.hk/en/collection/makers/theresa-hak-kyung-cha/.

Clare, Eli. *Brilliant Imperfection: Grappling with Cure*. Duke University Press, 2017.

Clark, Emily Jeannine. "'Their Negro Nanny was with Child By a White Man': Gossip, Sex, and Slavery in an Eighteenth-Century New England Town." *The William and Mary Quarterly* 79, no. 4 (2022): 533–62.

Claycomb, Ryan. *Lives in Play: Autobiography and Biography on the Feminist Stage*. University of Michigan Press, 2014.

Clements, Jennifer. "How Science Fiction Helps Us Reimagine Our Moral Relations with Animals." *Journal of Animal Ethics* 5, no. 2 (2015): 181–87.

Collins, Louise. "Gossip: A Feminist Defense." In *Good Gossip*. Edited by Robert F. Goodman and Aaron Ben-Ze'ev. University Press of Kansas, 1994.

Collins, Patricia Hill. *Black Feminist Thought: Knowledge, Consciousness, and the Politics of Empowerment*. Routledge Classics, 1990.

Danchev, Alex. *Magritte: A Life*. Profile Books Ltd., 2021.

Darwin, Charles. *The Expression of the Emotions in Man and Animals.* University of Chicago Press, 1965.

de Beauvoir, Simone. *A Very Easy Death.* Fitzcarraldo Editions, 2023.

DeMello, Margo. *Animals and Society: An Introduction to Human-Animal Studies.* Columbia University Press, 2012.

Derrida, Jacques. *The Animal That Therefore I Am.* Edited by Marie-Louise Mallet. Translated by David Wells. Fordham University Press, 2010.

Despentes, Virginie. "You Can't Rape a Woman Who's a Total Slut." *King Kong Theory.* Translated by Frank Wynne. FSG Originals, 2021.

Duffy, Jim. "Blue Bloods." *Johns Hopkins Magazine*, Summer 2021. https://hub.jhu.edu/magazine/2021/summer/horseshoe-crabs-covid19-medical-uses/.

Dungy, Camille T. *Guidebook to Relative Strangers: Journeys into Race, Motherhood, and History.* W.W. Norton, 2018.

Eisner, Chiara. "Coastal biomedical labs are bleeding more horseshoe crabs with little accountability." *NPR*, June 30, 2023.

Elkin, Lauren. *Art Monsters: Unruly Bodies in Feminist Art.* Farrar, Straus, and Giroux, 2023.

Elliott, T. J., and Gillian Tyler. *A Medieval Bestiary.* Godine, 1971.

Ellis, Bill. "Why Is a Lucky Rabbit's Foot Lucky?" In *Lucifer Ascending: The Occult in Folklore and Popular Culture.* University Press of Kentucky, 2004.

Etter, Sarah Rose. *The Book of X.* Two Dollar Radio, 2019.

Federal Bureau of Investigation. *Crime in the United States 1997: Uniform Crime Reports.* https://ucr.fbi.gov/crime-in-the-u.s/1997/toc97.pdf.

Federal Bureau of Investigation. *Crime in the United States 2016.* https://ucr.fbi.gov/crime-in-the-u.s/2016/crime-in-the-u.s.-2016.

Foucault, Michel. "The Simplest of Pleasures." *Generation online.* https://www.generation-online.org/p/fp_foucault13.htm.

Gaard, Greta. "Toward a Queer Ecofeminism." *Hypatia* 12, no. 1 (1997): 114–37.

Garland-Thomson, Rosemarie, ed. "From Wonder to Error—A Genealogy of Freak Discourse." In *Freakery: Cultural Spectacles of the Extraordinary Body.* New York University, 1996.

Garland-Thomson, Rosemarie. *Staring: How We Look.* Oxford University Press, 2009.

Geary, James. *I Is an Other: The Secret Life of Metaphor and How it Shapes the Way We See the World.* Harper, 2011.

Geertz, Armin W. "Hopi Indian Witchcraft and Healing: On Good, Evil, and Gossip." *American Indian Quarterly* 35, no. 3 (2011): 372–93.

Gill, Pat. "The Monstrous Years: Teens, Slasher Films, and the Family." *Journal of Film and Video* 54, no. 4 (2002): 16–30.

Gqola, Pumla Dineo. *Female Fear Factory: Unravelling Patriarchy's Cultures of Violence.* Cassava Republic Press, 2022.

Groff, Lauren. "Flower Hunters." In *Florida.* Penguin Publishing, 2019.

Gumbs, Alexis Pauline. *Undrowned: Black Feminist Lessons from Marine Mammals.* AK Press, 2020.

Halberstam, Jack. *Wild Things: The Disorder of Desire.* Duke University Press, 2020.

Hemenway, David, and Sara J. Solnick. "The epidemiology of self-defense gun use: Evidence from the National Crime Victimization Surveys 2007–2011." *Preventive Medicine* 79 (2015): 22–27.

Hoang, Lily. *A Bestiary.* Cleveland State University Poetry Center, 2016.

Hockett, Charles. "The Origin of Speech." In *Human Communication: Language and its Psychobiological Bases, Scientific American,* 1982.

Hong, Cathy Park. *Minor Feelings: An Asian American Reckoning.* Random House Publishing, 2020.

hooks, bell. *Ain't I A Woman: Black Women and Feminism.* Routledge Press, 2014.

hooks, bell. "Eating the Other: Desire and Resistance." In *Black Looks: Race and Representation: Second Edition.* Routledge, 2014.

Hooper, T. (director). (1974). *The Texas Chain Saw Massacre* [Film]. Vortex, Inc.

Igielnik, Ruth, Scott Keeter, and Hannah Hartig. "Behind Biden's 2020 Victory." *Pew Research Center,* June 30, 2021. https://www.pewresearch.org/politics/2021/06/30/behind-bidens-2020-victory/.

Inzaurralde, Bastien. "This Linguist Studied the Way Trump Speaks for Two Years. Here's What She Found." *Washington Post,* July 7, 2017.

Jones, Bradley. "An examination of the 2016 electorate, based on validated voters." *Pew Research Center.* August 9, 2018. https://www.pewresearch.org/politics/2018/08/09/an-examination-of-the-2016-electorate-based-on-validated-voters/.

Judson, George. "A Commencement Is Also a Memorial For 8th Year in a Row; Mistaken Belief in Immortality Seems the Only Link in Deaths at a Connecticut High School." *New York Times*, June 24, 1996.

Justice, Daniel Heath. *Badger*. Reaktion Books, 2015.

Justice, Daniel Heath. *Why Indigenous Literatures Matter*. Wilfrid Laurier University Press, 2018.

Kern, Leslie. *Feminist City: Claiming Space in a Man-Made World*. Verso Books, 2020.

Kimmerer, Robin Wall. *Braiding Sweetgrass: Indigenous Wisdom, Scientific Knowledge, and the Teachings of Plants*. Milkweed Editions, 2013.

Kings, A.E. "Intersectionality and the Changing Face of Ecofeminism." *Ethics and the Environment* 22, no. 1 (2017): 63–87.

Kinnell, Galway. "The Bear." In *Three Books: Body Rags; Mortal Acts, Mortal Words; The Past*. Houghton Mifflin Harcourt Publishing, 1993.

Krawec, Patty. *Becoming Kin: An Indigenous Call to Unforgetting the Past and Reimagining Our Future*. Broadleaf Books, 2022.

Krieger, Alex. "'Grace Dwelling in It': The Romance of the Suburb." In *City on a Hill: Urban Idealism in America from the Puritans to the Present*. Harvard University Press, 2019.

Kvaran, Kara M. "'You're All Doomed!' A Socioeconomic Analysis of Slasher Films." *Journal of American Studies* 50, no. 4 (2016): 953–70.

Lara, María Pía. *Beyond the Public Sphere: Film and the Feminist Imaginary*. Northwestern University Press, 2020.

Lara, María Pía. "Habermas's Concept of the Public Sphere and the New Feminist Agenda." *Los Angeles Review of Books*. August 11, 2019. https://lareviewofbooks.org/article/habermass-concept-public-sphere-new-feminist-agenda/.

Leys, Ruth. *From Guilt to Shame: Auschwitz and After*. Princeton University Press, 2009.

Lussana, Sergio A. *My Brother Slaves: Friendship, Masculinity, and Resistance in the Antebellum South*. University Press of Kentucky, 2016.

Maclear, Kyo. *Unearthing: A Story of Tangled Love and Family Secrets*. Scribner, 2023.

Magritte, René. *The Collective Invention*. 1934. Oil on canvas, 116 x 73 cm. Private collection. https://cr.middlebury.edu/public/spanish/sp371/all_invention.html.

Magritte, René. *René Magritte: Selected Writings*. Edited by Kathleen Rooney and Eric Plattner. Translated by Jo Levy. University of Minnesota Press, 2016.

Manguso, Sarah. "Writing Postpartum: A Conversation Between Kate Zambreno and Sarah Manguso." *The Paris Review*, April 24, 2019. https://www.theparisreview.org/blog/2019/04/24/writing -postpartum-a-conversation-between-kate-zambreno-and-sarah -manguso/.

Mansouri, Mohamed. "Animal Metaphor and Cultural Bias: Implications for the Translator." *Translation Journal*. April 2015. https:// translationjournal.net/April-2015/animal-metaphor-and-cultural -bias-implications-for-the-translator.html.

Masson, Jeffrey Moussaieff, and Susan McCarthy. *When Elephants Weep: The Emotional Lives of Animals*. Delta, 1996.

Maynard, Robyn, and Leanne Betasamosake Simpson. *Rehearsals for Living*. Haymarket Books, 2022.

Mitchell, Kaye. "Conclusion: The Shame Is (Not) Over." In *Writing Shame: Gender, Contemporary Literature and Negative Affect*. Edinburgh University Press, 2020.

Moore, Anne Elizabeth. *Body Horror: Capitalism, Fear, Misogyny, Jokes*. Feminist Press, 2023.

Mulvey, Laura. "Visual Pleasure and Narrative Cinema." In *Feminist Film Theory: A Reader*, edited by Sue Thornham. Edinburgh University Press, 1999. http://www.jstor.org/stable/10.3366/j.ctvxcrtm8.10.

Nelson, Maggie. *The Art of Cruelty: A Reckoning*. W.W. Norton, 2012.

New Art Publications. "Dani and Sheilah ReStack by Leeza Meksin." *BOMB Magazine*, March 4, 2024.

Nezhukumatathil, Aimee. *World of Wonders: In Praise of Fireflies, Whale Sharks, and Other Astonishments*. Milkweed Editions, 2020.

Nijman, Jan, and Tom Clery. "The United States: Suburban Imaginaries and Metropolitan Realities." In *Suburban Governance: A Global View*. Edited by Pierre Hamel and Roger Keil. University of Toronto Press, 2015.

Nutt, Gina. *Night Rooms*. Two Dollar Radio, 2021.

O'Donnell, Paul E. "Entre Chien et Loup: A Study of French Animal Metaphors." *The French Review* 63, no. 3 (1990): 514–23.

Paci, Patrizia, Clara Mancini, and Bashar Nuseibeh. "The Case for Animal Privacy in the Design of Technologically Supported Environments." *Frontiers in Veterinary Science* 8 (2022). https://www.frontiersin.org/journals/veterinary-science/articles/10.3389/fvets.2021.784794/full.

Passarello, Elena. *Animals Strike Curious Poses*. Sarabande Books, 2017.

Patterson, Kristine B., and Thomas Runge. "Smallpox and the Native American." *The American Journal of the Medical Sciences* 323, no. 4 (2002): 216–22.

Pierce, Kent. "Revolutionary War prisoners with smallpox remembered in Milford." *News8.wtnh.com*, July 4, 2017.

Poe, Edgar Allan. "The Tell-Tale Heart." In *The Tell-Tale Heart and Other Writings*. Bantam Classics, 1983.

Prince, Francesca. "How Table Manners as We Know Them Were a Renaissance Invention." *History*, National Geographic: May 3, 2021. https://www.nationalgeographic.com/history/history-magazine/article/table-manners-renaissance-catherine-de-medici.

Probyn, Elspeth. *Blush: Faces of Shame*. University of Minnesota Press, 2005.

Probyn, Elspeth. *Eating the Ocean*. Duke University Press. 2016.

Rankine, Claudia. *Don't Let Me Be Lonely: An American Lyric*. Graywolf Press, 2004.

Rankine, Claudia. *Just Us: An American Conversation*. Graywolf Press, 2020.

Rezvani, Bijan. "Elephant Emotions." *Nature*, October 24, 2014. https://pbs.org/wnet/nature/unforgettable-elephants-elephant-emotions/5886.

Ross, Sabrina N. "The Politics of Politeness: Theorizing Race, Gender, and Education in White Southern Space." *Counterpoints* 412 (2013): 143–159.

Rubenhold, Hallie. "5 Things You Didn't Know About the Women Killed by Jack the Ripper." February, 2019. https://www.penguin.co.uk/articles/2019/02/things-you-didn-t-know-about-the-women-killed-by-jack-the-ripper.

Rutherford, Stephanie. *Villain, Vermin, Icon, Kin: Wolves and the Making of Canada*. McGill- Queen's University Press, 2022.

Ryan, Derek. "Animal Ontology." In *Animal Theory: A Critical Introduction*. Edinburgh University Press, 2015.

Sartre, Jean-Paul. "The Existence of Others." In *Being and Nothingness: An Essay in Phenomenological Ontology*. Citadel Press, 1956.

Schiebinger, Londa. *Nature's Body: Gender in the Making of Modern Science*. Beacon Press, 1993.

Sclafani, Jennifer. "The Idiolect of Donald Trump." *Scientific American*, March 25, 2016. https://www.scientificamerican.com/blog/mind-guest-blog/the-idiolect-of-donald-trump/.

Sedgwick, Eve Kosofsky. *Touching Feeling: Affect, Pedagogy, Performativity*. Duke University Press, 2002.

She, Megan. "Resisting Nonperformativity: Emma Sulkowicz's Challenges to Victimhood," *Johns Hopkins Theatre Journal* 75, no. 1 (2023): 19–39.

Shelley, Mary. *Frankenstein; or The Modern Prometheus*. Prestwick House, 2005.

Simpson, Leanne Betasamosake. *As We Have Always Done: Indigenous Freedom Through Radical Resistance*. University of Minnesota Press, 2017.

Sinclair, Upton. *The Jungle*. Edited by Clare Virginia Eby. W.W. Norton, 2003.

Spiegel, Marjorie. *The Dreaded Comparison: Human and Animal Slavery*. Mirror Books, 1997.

St. Clair, Kassia. *The Secret Lives of Color*. Penguin Books, 2016.

Suddendorf, Thomas. *The Gap: The Science of What Separates Us From Other Animals*. Basic Books, 2013.

TallBear, Kim. "Disrupting Settlement, Sex, and Nature." Transcript via Indigenous Futures, n.d. https://indigenousfutures.net/wp-content/uploads/2016/10/Kim_TallBear.pdf.

Tatar, Maria. *The Heroine with 1001 Faces*. Liveright, 2021.

Thrasher, Steven W. *Black Suburbia: From Levittown to Ferguson*, June 2016. Schomburg Center for Research in Black Culture, New York Public Library. Accessed August, 2023. https://nypl.org/events/exhibitions/black-suburbia-levittown-ferguson.

Todd, Zoe. "An Indigenous Feminist's Take On The Ontological Turn: 'Ontology' Is Just Another Word For Colonialism." *Journal of Historical Sociology* 29, no. 1 (2016): 4–22.

Uganda Wildlife Authority. "Rhino: Uganda Wildlife Authority." Uganda Wildlife Authority - Conserving Uganda's Wildlife for Generations. Accessed June 19, 2022. https://ugandawildlife.org/animals/rhino.

Umland, Anne, ed. *Magritte: The Mystery of the Ordinary, 1926–1938*. MoMA, 2014.

Vyse, Stuart. *Superstition: A Very Short Introduction*. Oxford University Press, 2020.

Ward, Frazer. *No Innocent Bystanders: Performance Art and Audience*. Dartmouth College Press, 2012.

Weber, Paul J. and Jamie Stengle. "Kate Cox sought an abortion in Texas. A court said no because she didn't show her life was in danger." *AP News*, December 12, 2023.

White, Artress Bethany. *Survivor's Guilt: Essays on Race and American Identity*. New Rivers Press, 2022.

Books in the Life Writing Series

Published by Wilfrid Laurier University Press

Tracing the Autobiographical edited by Marlene Kadar, Linda Warley, Jeanne Perreault, and Susanna Egan • 2005 • viii + 280 pp. • ISBN 978-0-88920-476-8

Must Write: Edna Staebler's Diaries edited by Christl Verduyn • 2005 • viii + 304 pp. • ISBN 978-0-88920-481-2

Pursuing Giraffe: A 1950s Adventure by Anne Innis Dagg • 2006 • xvi + 284 pp. • 46 b&w photos, 2 maps • ISBN 978-0-88920-463-8

Food That Really Schmecks by Edna Staebler • 2007 • xxiv + 334 pp. • ISBN 978-0-88920-521-5

163256: A Memoir of Resistance by Michael Englishman • 2007 • xvi + 112 pp. • 14 b&w photos • ISBN 978-1-55458-009-5

The Wartime Letters of Leslie and Cecil Frost, 1915–1919 edited by R.B. Fleming • 2007 • xxxvi + 384 pp. • 49 b&w photos, 5 maps • ISBN 978-1-55458-470-3

Johanna Krause Twice Persecuted: Surviving in Nazi Germany and Communist East Germany by Carolyn Gammon and Christiane Hemker • 2007 • x + 170 pp. • 58 b&w photos, 2 maps • ISBN 978-1-55458-006-4

Watermelon Syrup: A Novel by Annie Jacobsen with Jane Finlay-Young and Di Brandt • 2007 • x + 268 pp. • ISBN 978-1-55458-005-7

Broad Is the Way: Stories from Mayerthorpe by Margaret Norquay • 2008 • x + 106 pp. • 6 b&w photos • ISBN 978-1-55458-020-0

Becoming My Mother's Daughter: A Story of Survival and Renewal by Erika Gottlieb • 2008 • x + 178 pp. • 53 colour and b&w illus. • ISBN 978-1-55458-030-9

Leaving Fundamentalism: Personal Stories edited by G. Elijah Dann • 2008 • xii + 234 pp. • ISBN 978-1-55458-026-2

Bearing Witness: Living with Ovarian Cancer edited by Kathryn Carter and Lauri Elit • 2009 • viii + 94 pp. • ISBN 978-1-55458-055-2

Dead Woman Pickney: A Memoir of Childhood in Jamaica by Yvonne Shorter Brown • 2010 • viii + 202 pp. • ISBN 978-1-55458-189-4

I Have a Story to Tell You by Seemah C. Berson • 2010 • xx + 288 pp. • 24 b&w photos • ISBN 978-1-55458-219-8

We All Giggled: A Bourgeois Family Memoir by Thomas O. Hueglin • 2010 • xiv + 232 pp. • 20 b&w photos • ISBN 978-1-55458-262-4

Just a Larger Family: Letters of Marie Williamson from the Canadian Home Front, 1940–1944 edited by Mary F. Williamson and Tom Sharp • 2011 • xxiv + 378 pp. • 16 b&w photos • ISBN 978-1-55458-323-2

Burdens of Proof: Faith, Doubt, and Identity in Autobiography by Susanna Egan • 2011 • x + 200 pp. • ISBN 978-1-55458-333-1

Accident of Fate: A Personal Account 1938–1945 by Imre Rochlitz with Joseph Rochlitz • 2011 • xiv + 226 pp. • 50 b&w photos, 5 maps • ISBN 978-1-55458-267-9

The Green Sofa by Natascha Würzbach, translated by Raleigh Whitinger • 2012 • xiv + 240 pp. • 5 b&w photos • ISBN 978-1-55458-334-8

Unheard Of: Memoirs of a Canadian Composer by John Beckwith • 2012 • x + 394 pp. • 74 b&w illus., 8 musical examples • ISBN 978-1-55458-358-4

Borrowed Tongues: Life Writing, Migration, and Translation by Eva C. Karpinski • 2012 • viii + 274 pp. • ISBN 978-1-55458-357-7

Basements and Attics, Closets and Cyberspace: Explorations in Canadian Women's Archives edited by Linda M. Morra and Jessica Schagerl • 2012 • x + 338 pp. • ISBN 978-1-77112-328-0

The Memory of Water by Allen Smutylo • 2013 • x + 262 pp. • 65 colour illus. • ISBN 978-1-55458-842-8

The Unwritten Diary of Israel Unger, Revised Edition by Carolyn Gammon and Israel Unger • 2013 • x + 230 pp. • 90 b&w illus. • ISBN 978-1-77112-011-1

Boom!: Manufacturing Memoir for the Popular Market by Julie Rak • 2013 • viii + 250 pp. • 7 b&w illus. • ISBN 978-1-55458-939-5

Motherlode: A Mosaic of Dutch Wartime Experience by Carolyne Van Der Meer • 2014 • xiv + 132 pp. • 6 b&w illus. • ISBN 978-1-77112-005-0

Not the Whole Story: Challenging the Single Mother Narrative edited by Lea Caragata and Judit Alcalde • 2014 • x + 222 pp. • ISBN 978-1-55458-624-0

Street Angel by Magie Dominic • 2014 • viii + 154 pp. • ISBN 978-1-77112-026-5

In the Unlikeliest of Places: How Nachman Libeskind Survived the Nazis, Gulags, and Soviet Communism by Annette Libeskind Berkovits with a foreword by Daniel Libeskind • 2014 • xiv + 282 pp. • 6 colour illus. • ISBN 978-1-77112-066-1

Kinds of Winter: Four Solo Journeys by Dogteam in Canada's Northwest Territories by Dave Olesen • 2014 • xii + 256 pp. • 17 b&w illus., 6 maps • ISBN 978-1-77112-131-6